CW00322161

CONTENTS

Key to Map Pages............ 2-3
Road Maps.....................4-42
Index to Towns and Villages...........43-55
Town Plans, Airport & Port Plans...56-60

REFERENCE

MOTORWAY	**M1**
Under Construction	
Proposed	
MOTORWAY JUNCTIONS WITH NUMBERS	
Unlimited interchange **6** Limited interchange **7**	
MOTORWAY SERVICE AREA	**SOUTH MIMMS**
with access from one carriageway only	Ⓢ
MAJOR ROAD SERVICE AREAS	**BABRAHAM**
with 24 hour Facilities	Ⓢ
PRIMARY ROUTE _ (with junction number)	**61** **A14**
PRIMARY ROUTE DESTINATION	**DISS**
DUAL CARRIAGEWAYS (A & B Roads)	
CLASS A ROAD	A143
CLASS B ROAD	B1113
MAJOR ROADS UNDER CONSTRUCTION	
MAJOR ROADS PROPOSED	
GRADIENT 1:5(20%) & STEEPER (Ascent in direction of arrow)	≪
TOLL	TOLL
MILEAGE BETWEEN MARKERS	8
RAILWAY AND STATION	
LEVEL CROSSING AND TUNNEL	
RIVER OR CANAL	
COUNTY OR UNITARY AUTHORITY BOUNDARY	
NATIONAL BOUNDARY	+
BUILT-UP AREA	
VILLAGE OR HAMLET	○
WOODED AREA	
SPOT HEIGHT IN FEET	• 813
HEIGHT ABOVE 400' - 1,000' 122m - 305m	
SEA LEVEL 1,000' - 1,400' 305m - 427m	
1,400' - 2,000' 427m - 610m	
2,000'+ 610m +	
NATIONAL GRID REFERENCE (Kilometres)	100
AREA COVERED BY TOWN PLAN	**SEE PAGE 57**

TOURIST INFORMATION

AIRPORT	✈
AIRFIELD	✈
HELIPORT	
BATTLE SITE AND DATE	✕ 1066
CASTLE (Open to Public)	
CASTLE WITH GARDEN (Open to Public)	
CATHEDRAL, ABBEY, CHURCH, FRIARY, PRIORY	✝
COUNTRY PARK	
FERRY (Vehicular)	
(Foot only)	
GARDEN (Open to Public)	
GOLF COURSE _____ 9 HOLE 18 HOLE	
HISTORIC BUILDING (Open to Public)	
HISTORIC BUILDING WITH GARDEN (Open to Public)	
HORSE RACECOURSE	
INFORMATION CENTRE	🄸
LIGHTHOUSE	
MOTOR RACING CIRCUIT	
MUSEUM, ART GALLERY	
NATIONAL PARK OR FOREST PARK	
NATIONAL TRUST PROPERTY (Open)	NT
(Restricted Opening)	NT
NATURE RESERVE OR BIRD SANCTUARY	
NATURE TRAIL OR FOREST WALK	
PLACE OF INTEREST Monument	•
PICNIC SITE	
RAILWAY, STEAM OR NARROW GAUGE	
THEME PARK	
VIEWPOINT _____ 360 degrees	
180 degrees	
WILDLIFE PARK	
WINDMILL	
ZOO OR SAFARI PARK	

SCALE

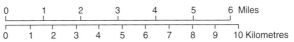

1:158,400
2.5 Miles to 1 Inch

Geographers' A-Z Map Company Ltd

Fairfield Road, Borough Green,
Sevenoaks, Kent TN15 8PP

01732 781000 (Enquiries & Trade Sales)
01732 783422 (Retail Sales)

Edition 8 2006
Copyright © Geographers' A-Z Map Company Ltd.

www.a-zmaps.co.uk

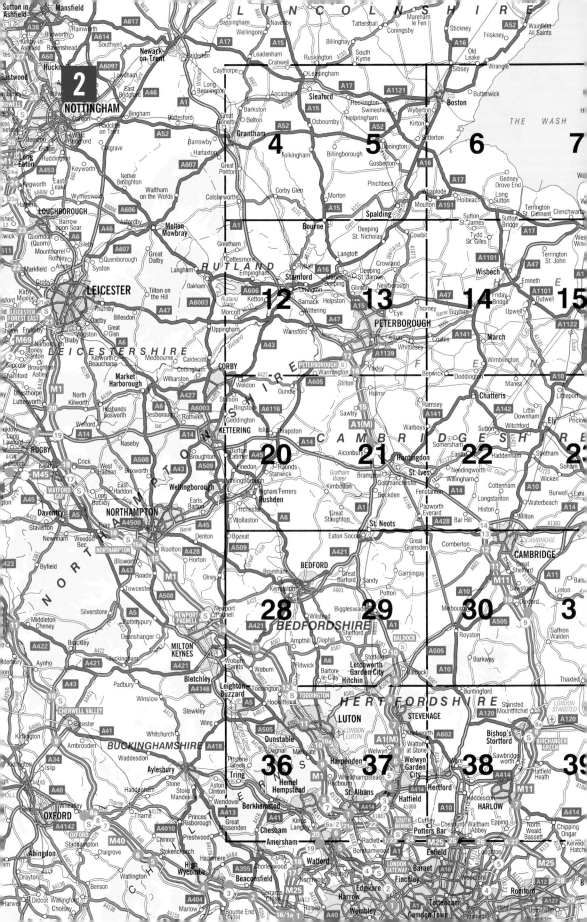

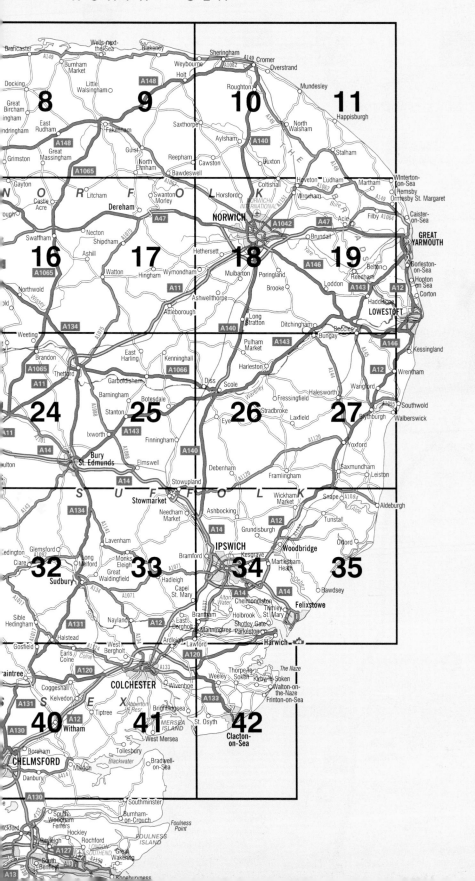

NORTH SEA

3

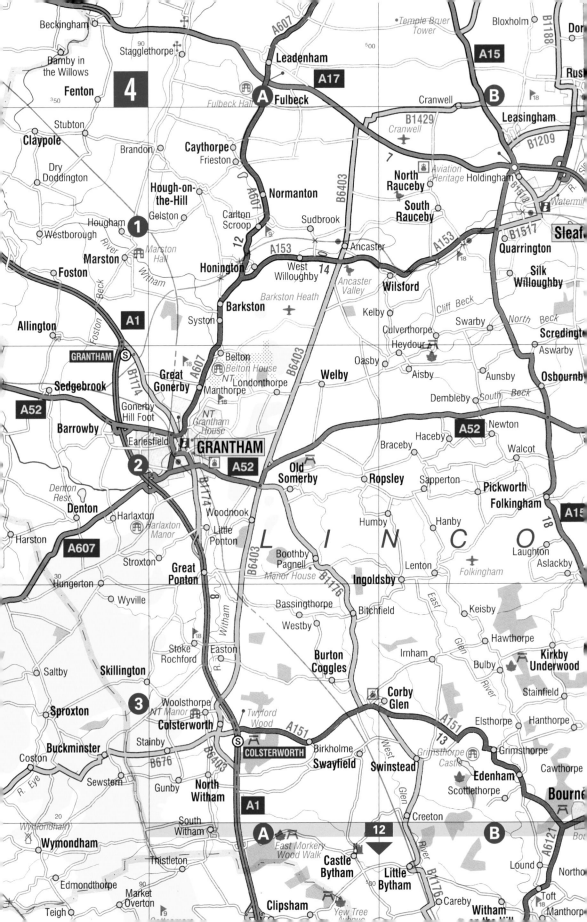

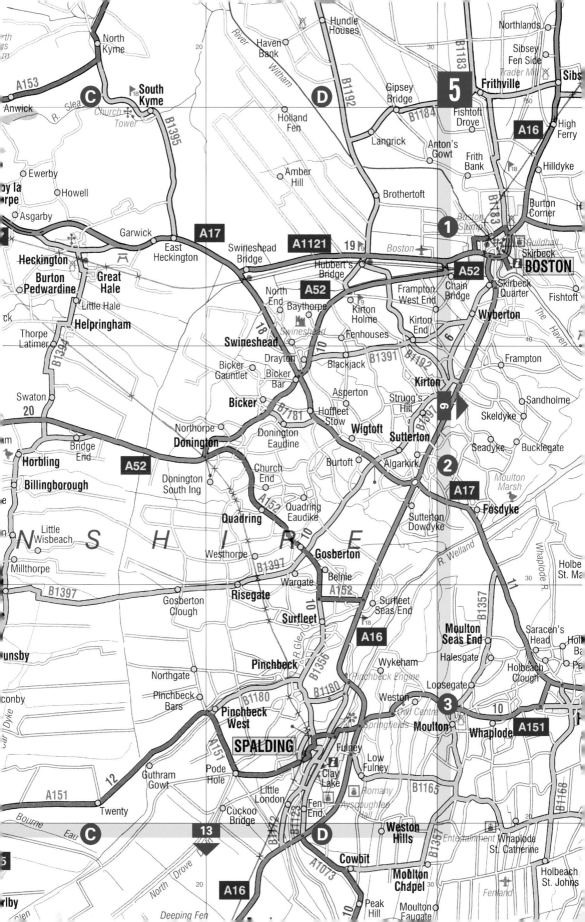

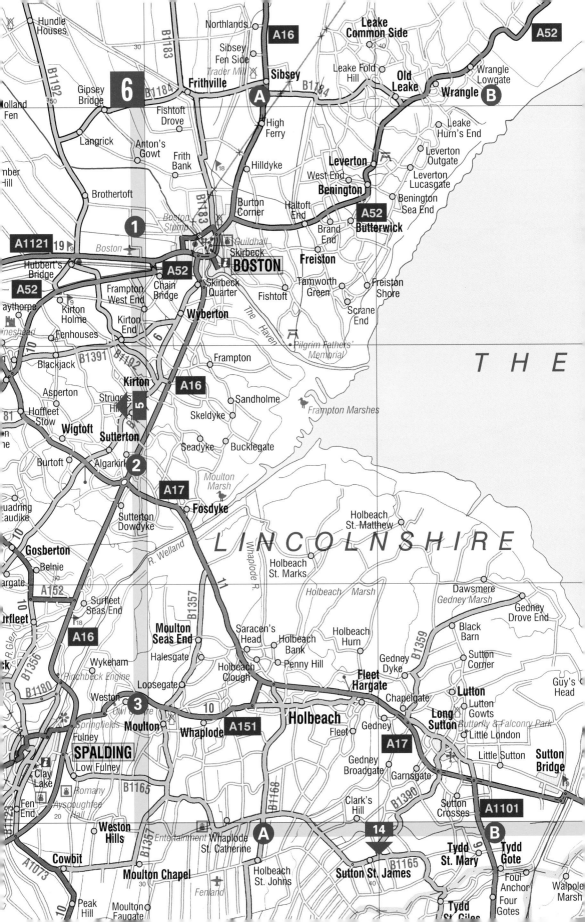

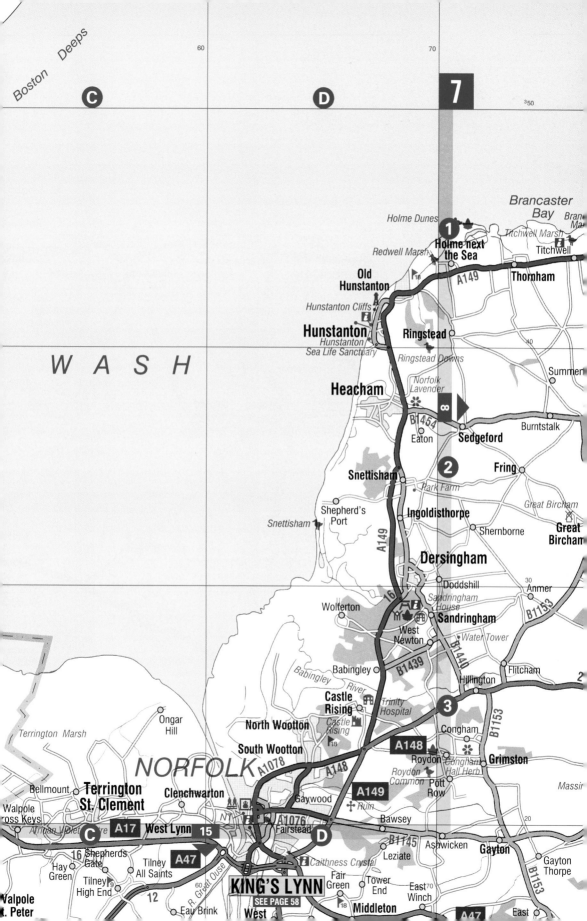

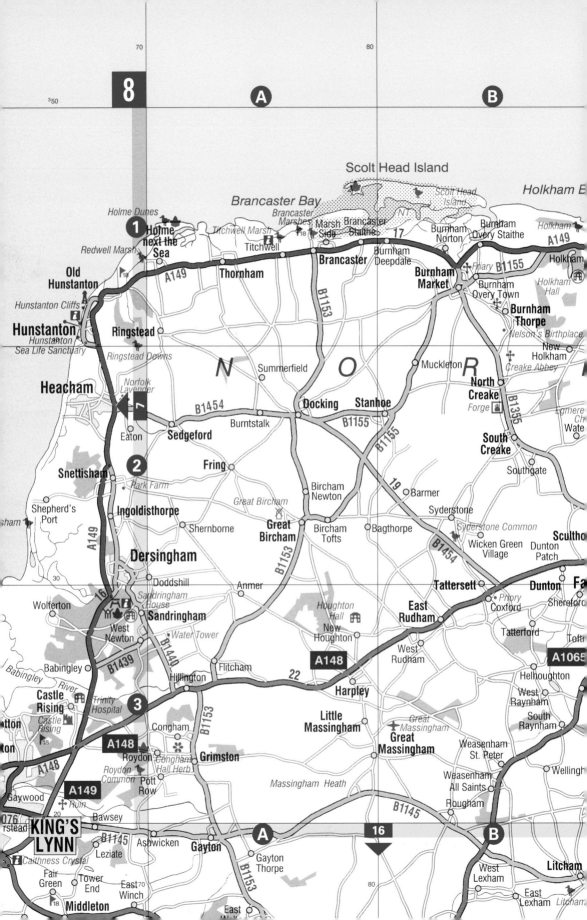

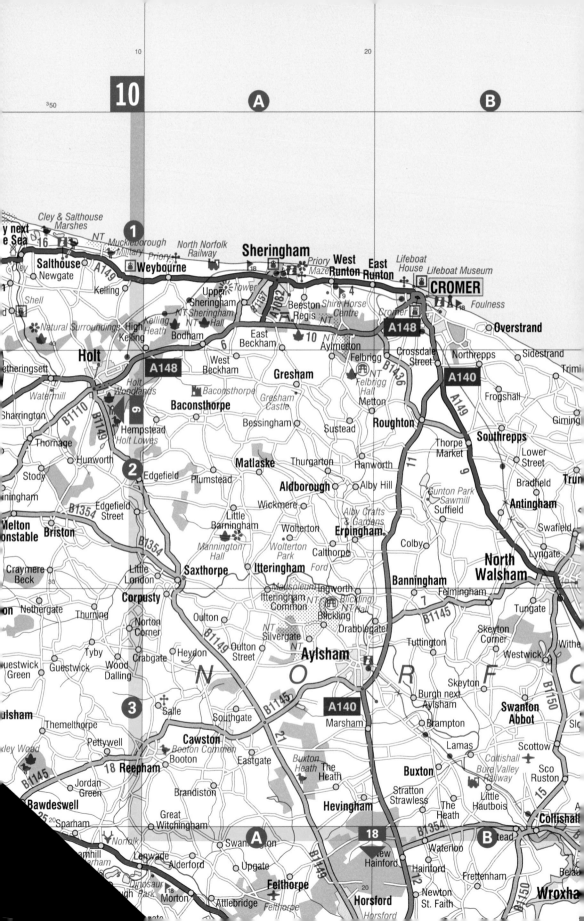

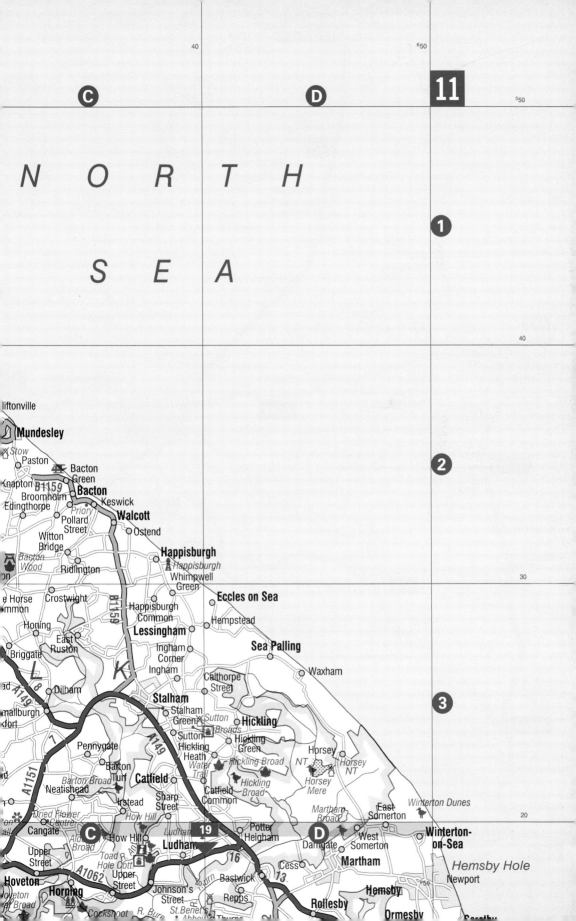

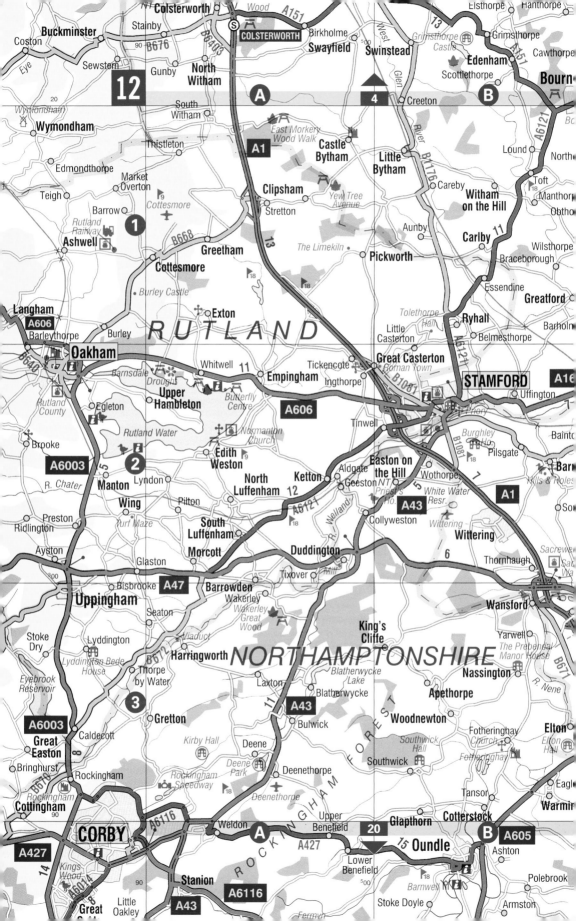

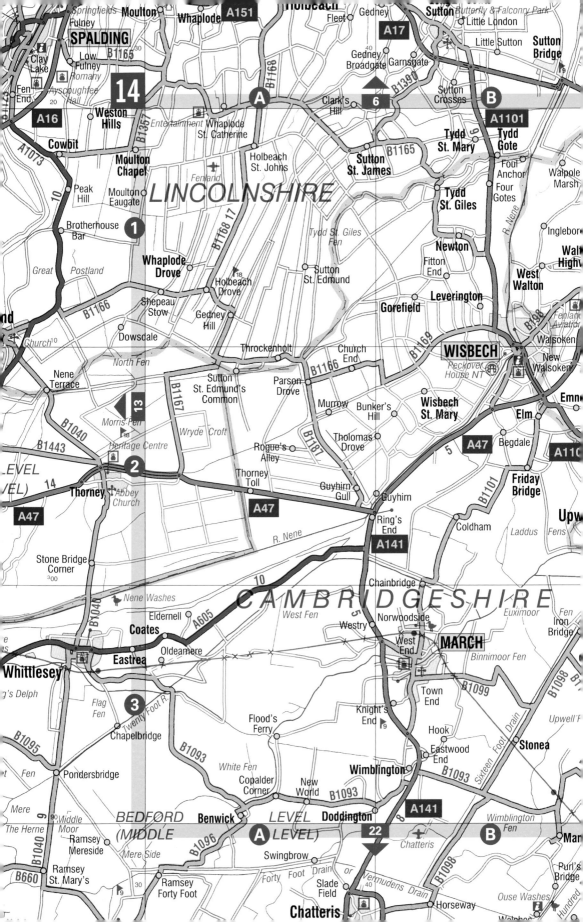

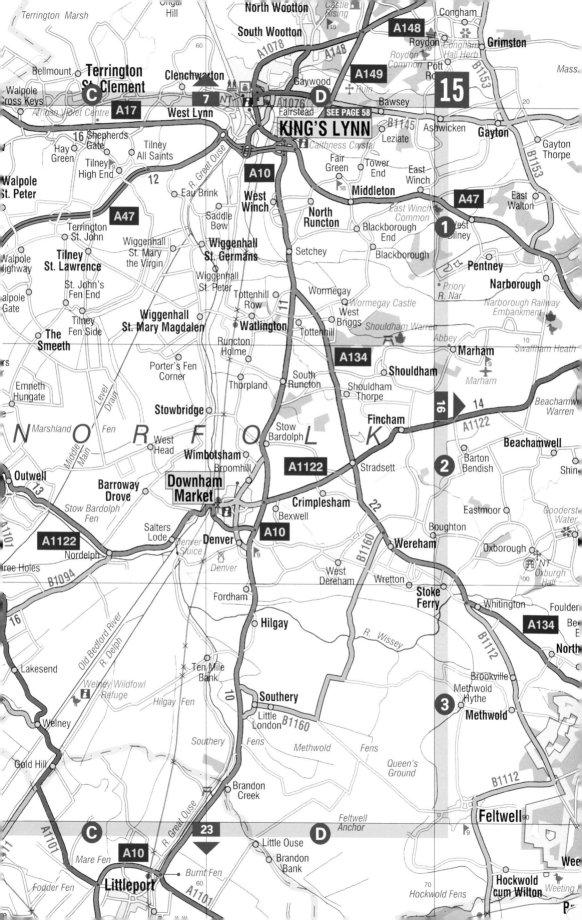

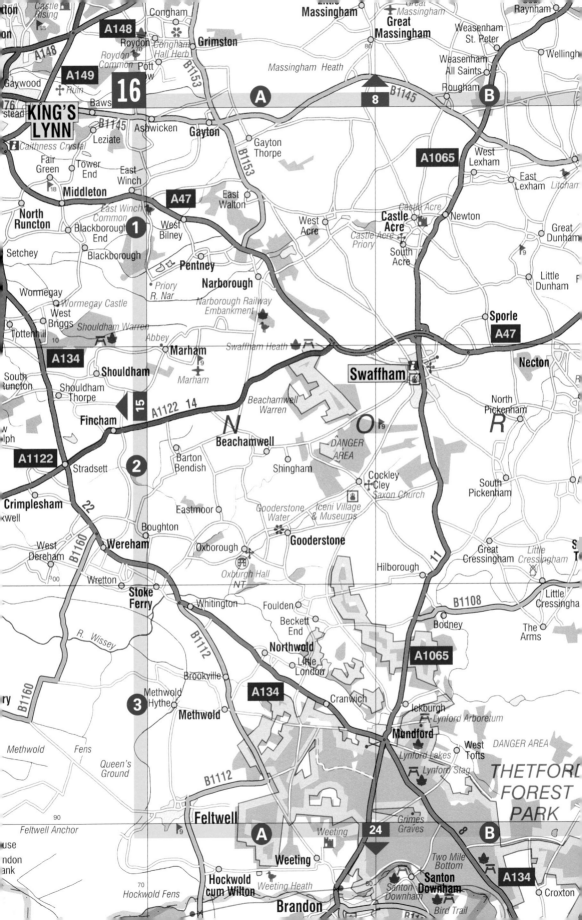

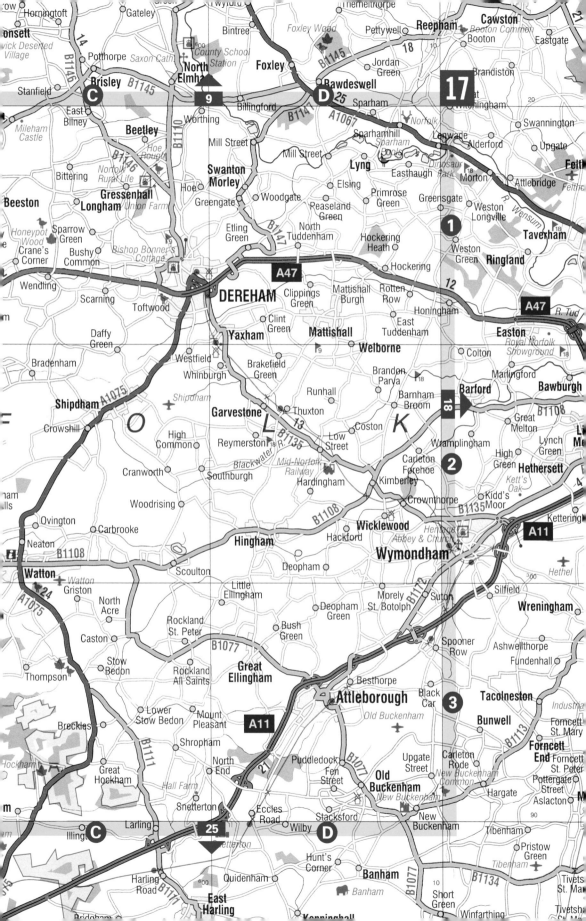

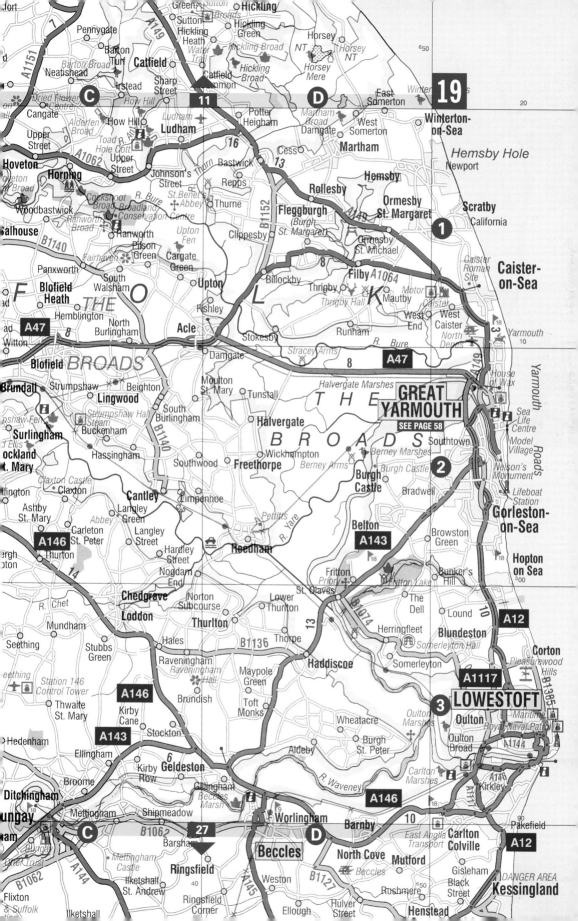

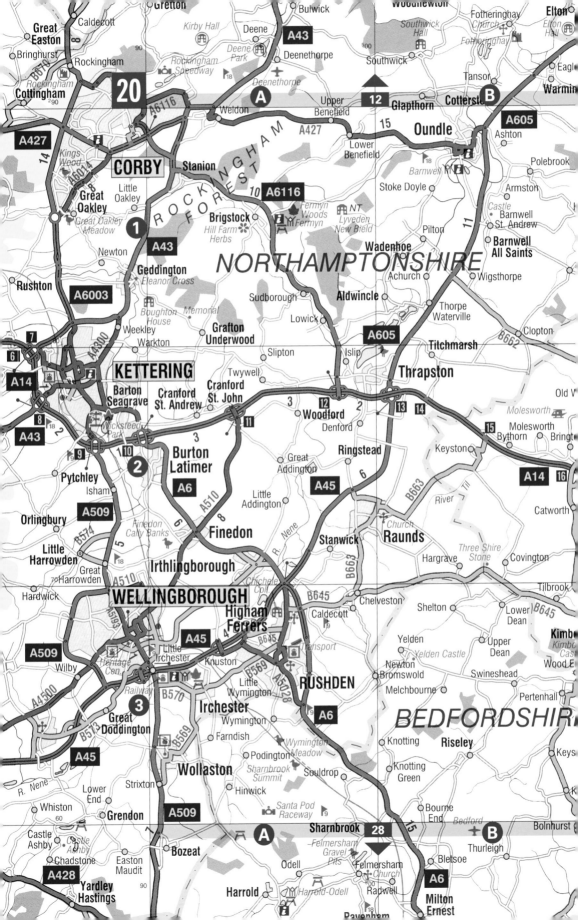

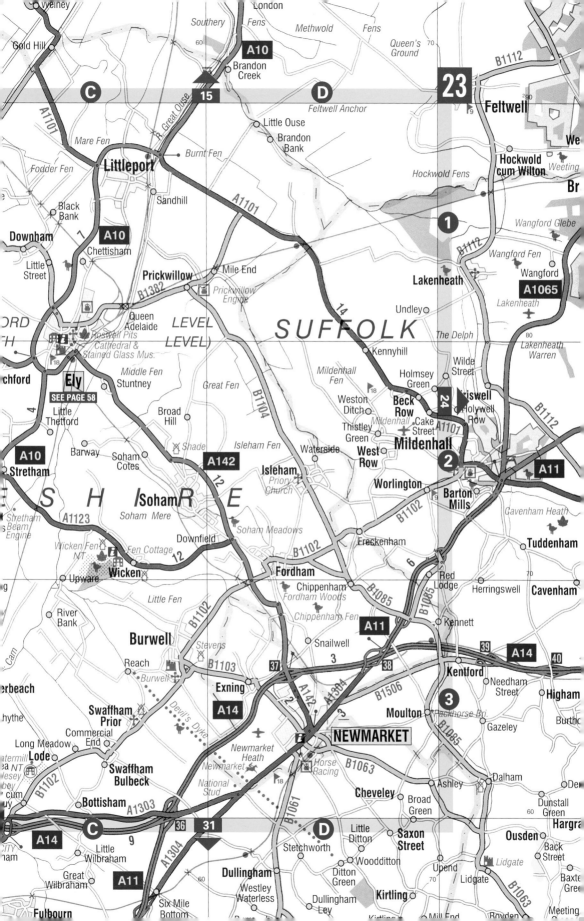

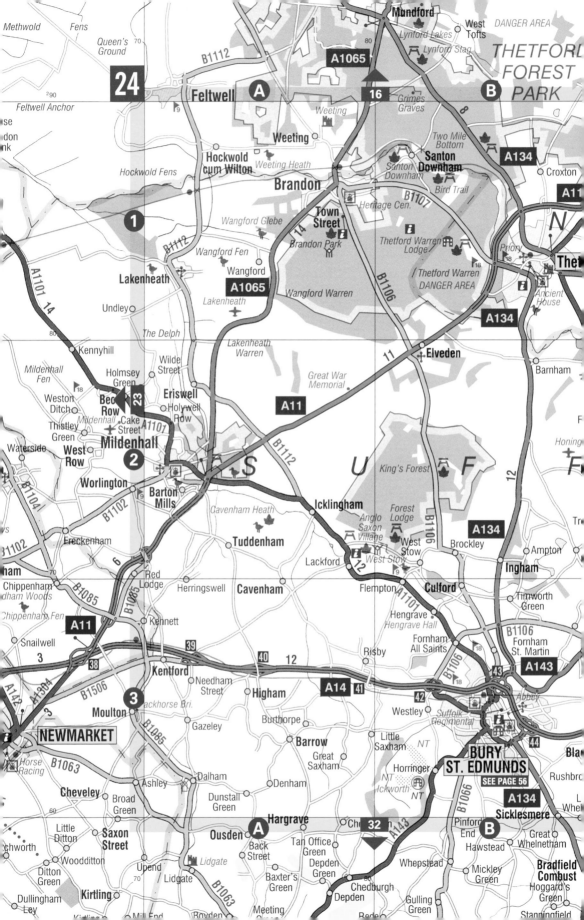

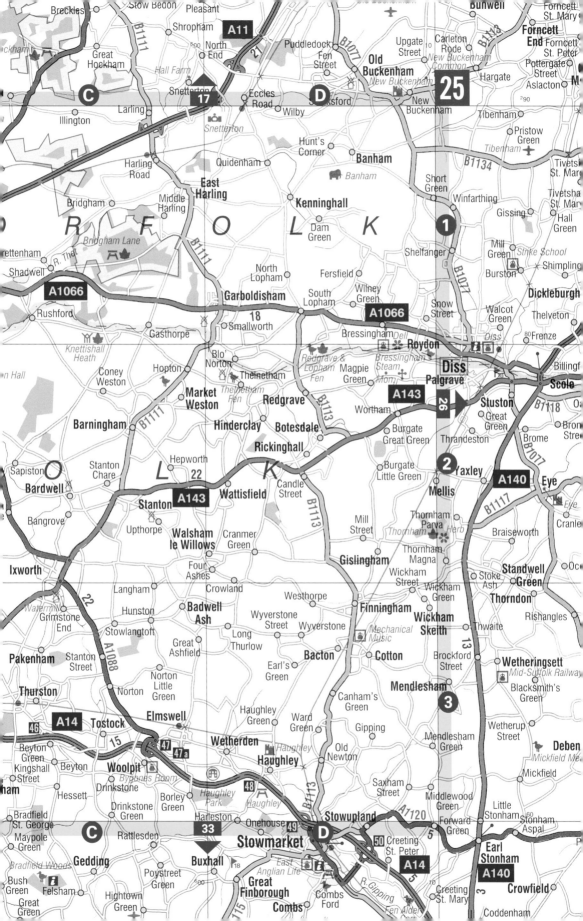

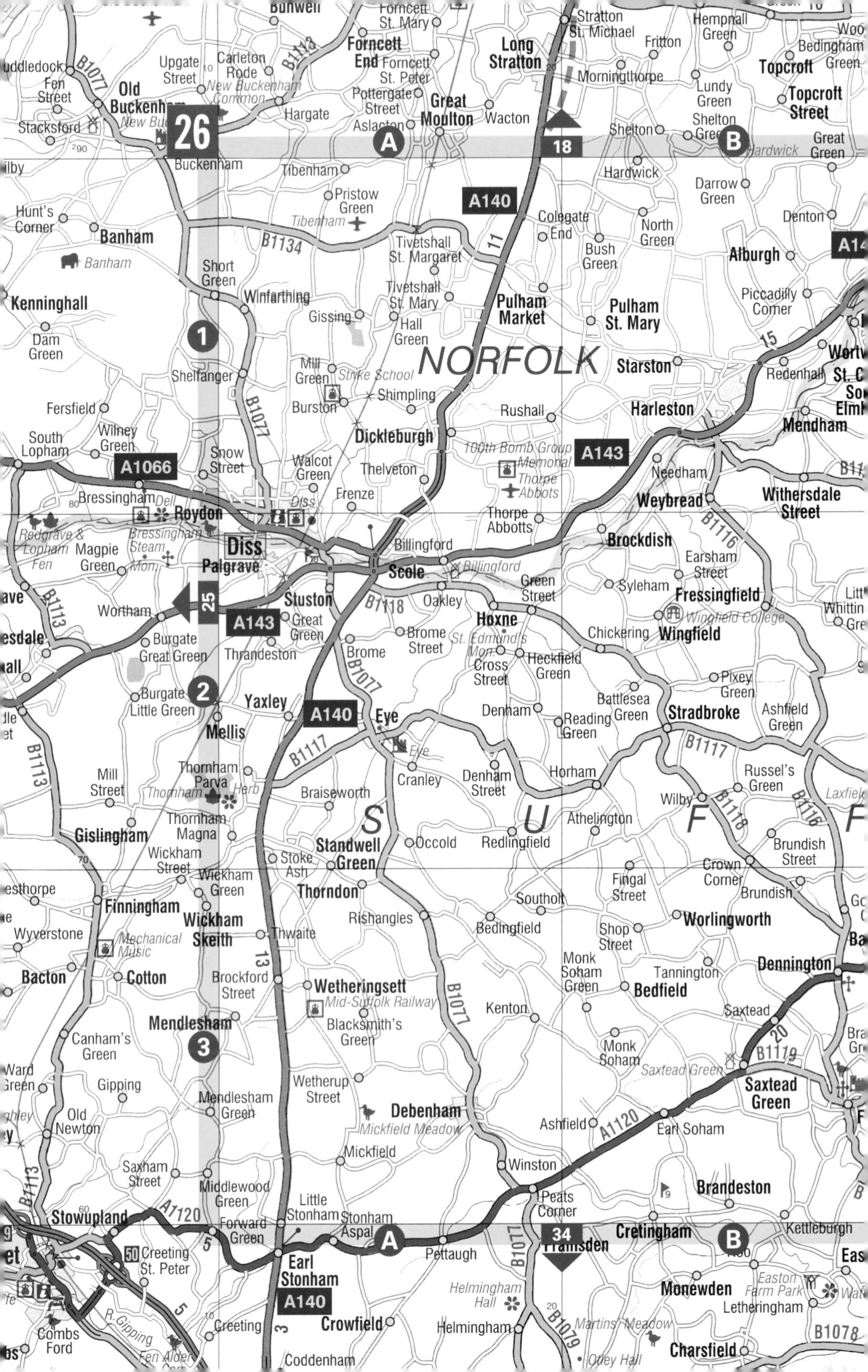

Bunwell

Forncett St. Mary

Stratton St. Michael

Hempnall Green

Woo

B1077

Upgate Street

Carleton Rode

Forncett End

Forncett St. Peter

Long Stratton

Fritton

Bedingham Green

uddleddock
Fen Street

New Buckenham Common

Hargate

Pottergate Street

Great Moulton

Wacton

Morningthorpe

Topcroft

Topcroft Street

Old Buckenham

26

A

Aslacton

18

Shelton

Lundy Green

Shelton Green

Great Green

Stacksford

New Bu

290

Buckenham

Tibenham

A140

Hardwick

Hardwick

Darrow Green

Banham

B1134

Pristow Green

Tibenham

11

Colegate End

Bush Green

North Green

Denton

Alburgh

A14

Banham

Short Green

Tivetshall St. Margaret

Tibenham

Piccadilly Corner

Kenninghall

Winfarthing

B1077

Tivetshall St. Mary

Gissing

Hall Green

NORFOLK

Starston

15

Redenhall

Wortw St. C Sou Elm

Dam Green

Shelfanger

Mill Green

Strike School

Shimpling

Pulham Market

Pulham St. Mary

Harleston

Mendham

Fersfield

Burston

Rushall

South Lopham

Wilney Green

Snow Street

Walcot Green

Thelveton

Dickleburgh

100th Bomb Group Memorial Thorpe Abbots

A143

Needham

Weybread

Withersdale Street

A1066

Bressingham

Dell

Frenze

Thorpe Abbotts

Brockdish

Earsham Street

B11

Redgrave & Lopham Fen

80

Magpie Green

Bressingham Steam

Mom

Roydon

Diss

Diss

Palgrave

Billingford

Scole

Billingford

Green Street

Syleham

Fressingfield

Wingfield College

Wingfield

wave

B1113

Wortham

25

A143

Stuston

Great Green

B1118

Oakley

Hoxne

St. Edmund's Mon

Chickering

esdale

Burgate Great Green

Thrandeston

Brome

Brome Street

Cross Street

Heckfield Green

Battlesea Green

Stradbroke

Pixey Green

Ashfield Green

all

Burgate Little Green

2

Yaxley

A140

Eye

Denham

Reading Green

Horham

B1117

Russel's Green

dle et

Mellis

Eye

Cranley

Denham Street

Wilby

B1118

Laxfiel

F

Mill Street

Thornham Parva

Herb

Braiseworth

Athelington

B1116

Gislingham

Thornham Magna

Occold

Redlingfield

Brundish Street

70

Wickham Street

Standwell Green

Southolt

Fingal Street

Crown Corner

Brundish

Go

esthorpe

Finningham

Wickham Green

Stoke Ash

Thorndon

Rishangles

Bedingfield

Shop Street

Worlingworth

Ba

Wyverstone

Wickham Skeith

Thwaite

Monk Soham Green

Tannington

Dennington

Bacton

Cotton

Mechanical Music

Brockford Street

Wetheringsett

Mid-Suffolk Railway

Kenton

Bedfield

Saxtead

20

B1119

Canham's Green

Mendlesham

3

Blacksmith's Green

Monk Soham

Saxtead Green

Bra Gre

Gipping

Old Newton

Mendlesham Green

Wetherup Street

Debenham

Mickfield Meadow

Ashfield

Earl Soham

Saxtead Green

Brandeston

Ward Green

Saxham Street

Middlewood Green

Mickfield

Winston

A1120

B1113

Stowupland

A1120

5

Forward Green

Little Stonham

Stonham Aspal

Peats Corner

9

Kettleburgh

Eas

50

Creeting St. Peter

10

A

Pettaugh

B1077

34

Framsden

Cretingham

B

Monewden

Easton Farm Park

Wat

Earl Stonham

A140

Crowfield

Helmingham Hall

Helmingham

20

Martins Meadow

Monewden

Letheringham

Combs Ford

R. Gipping

Fen Alder

5

Greeting

3

Coddenham

B1079

Otley Hall

Charsfield

B1078

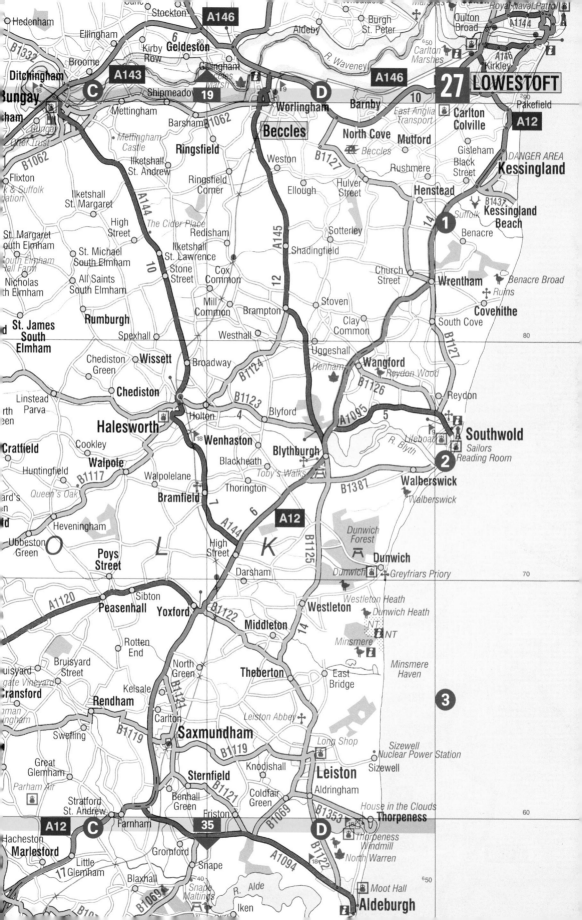

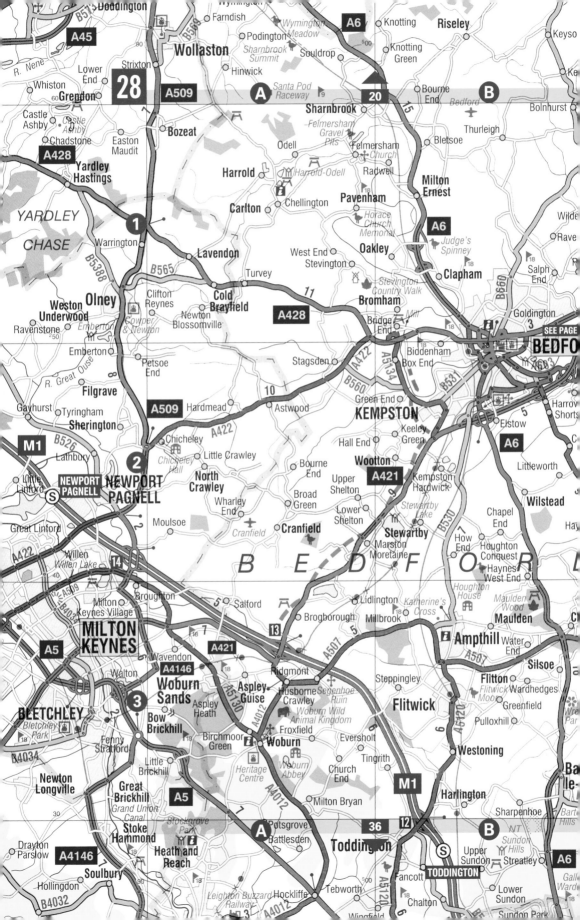

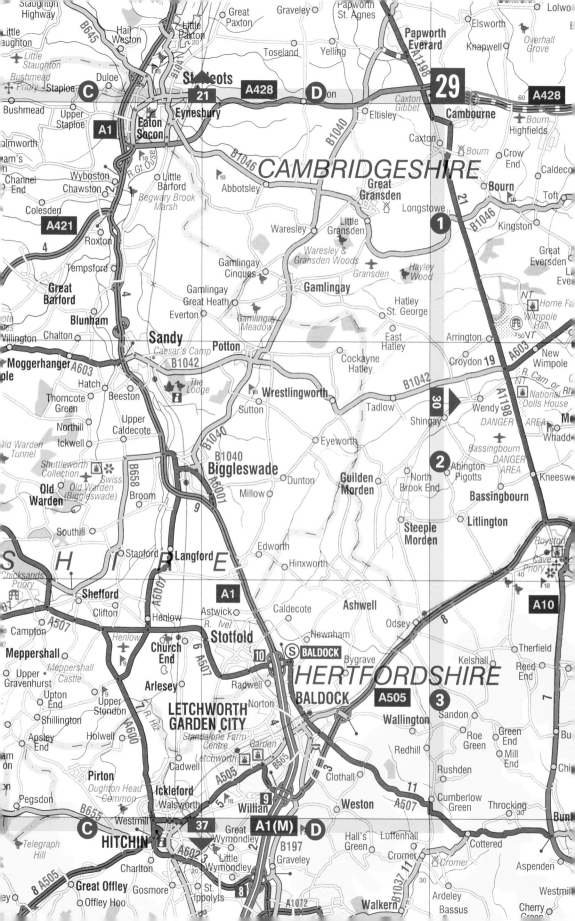

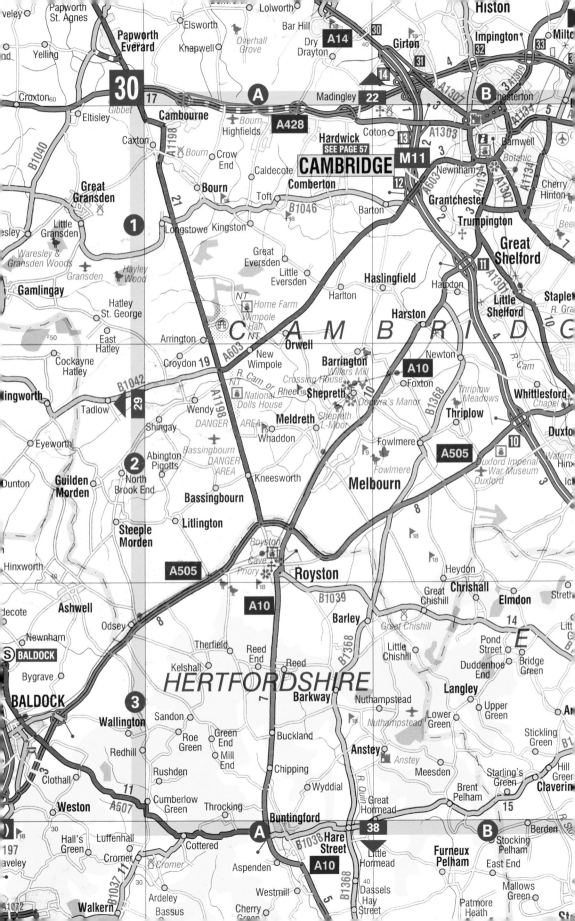

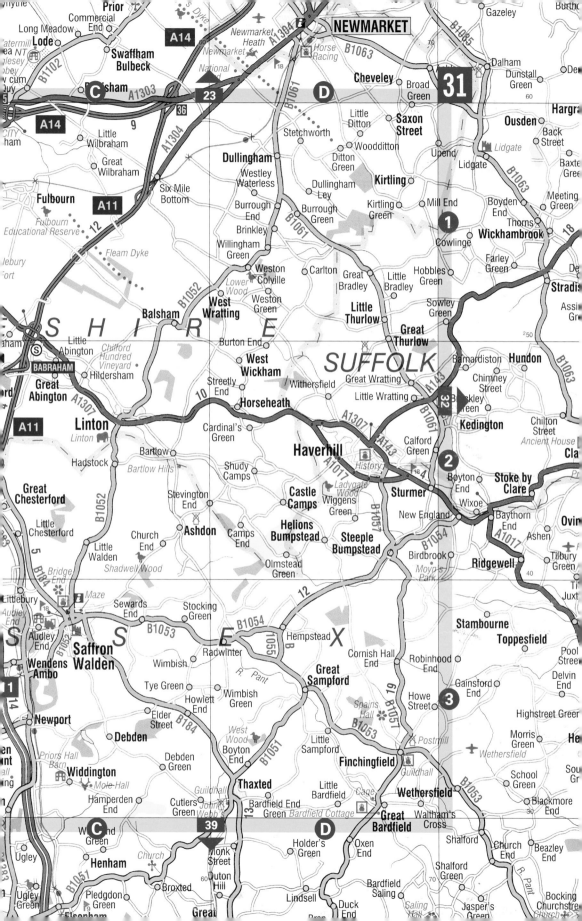

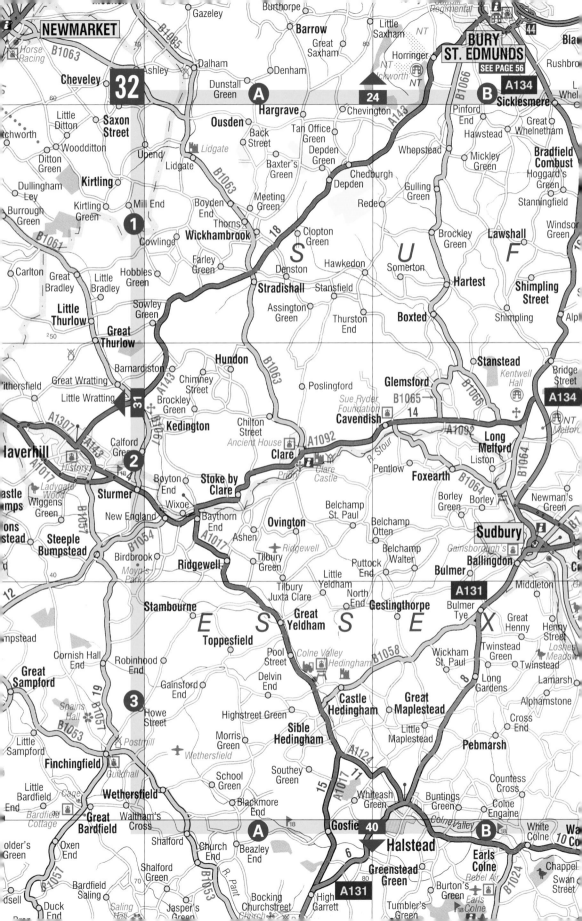

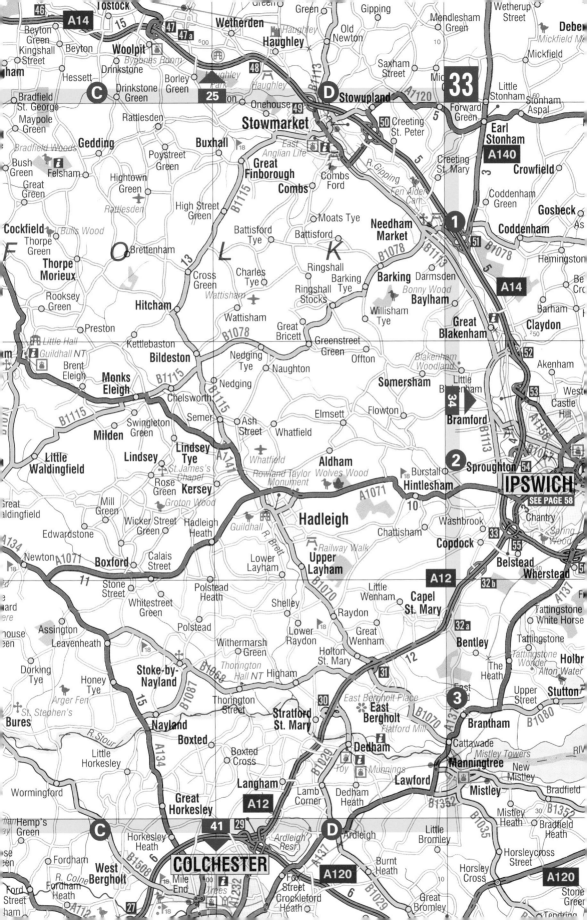

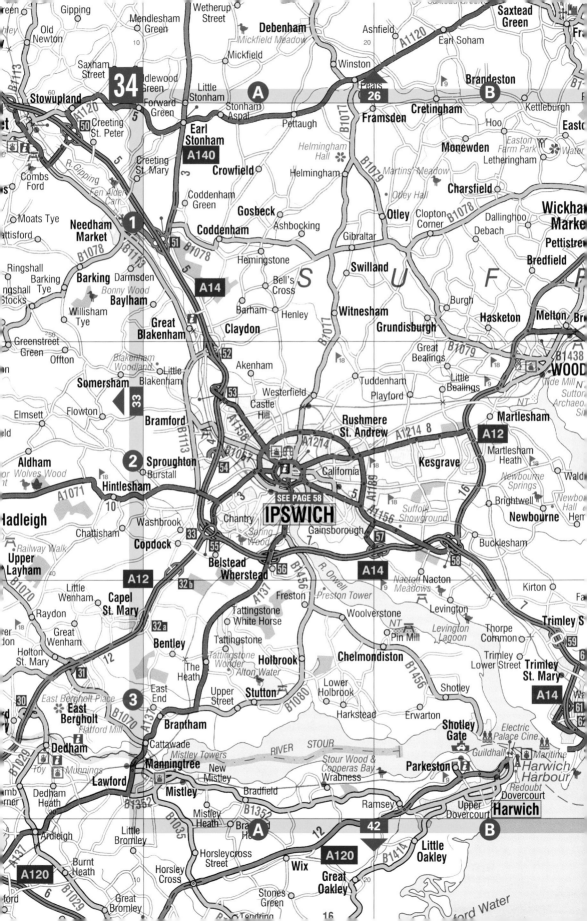

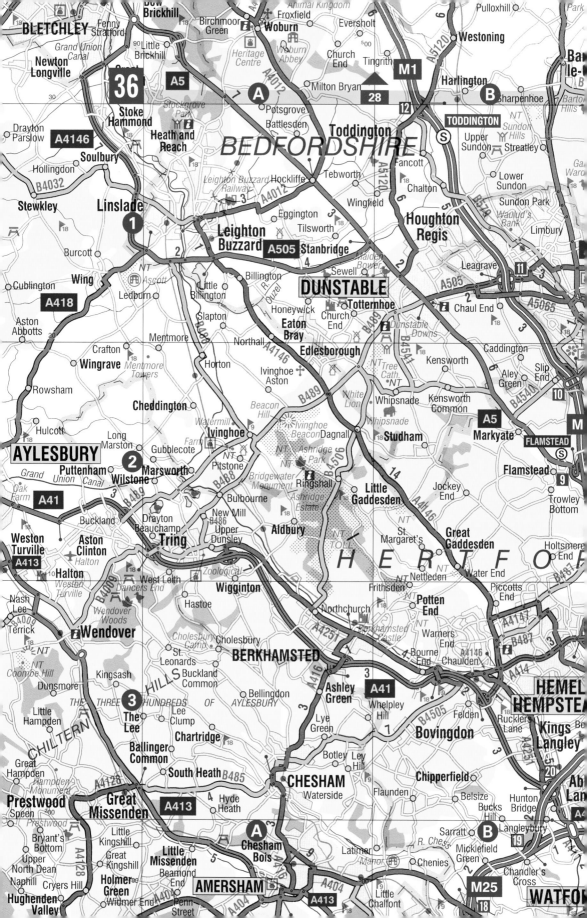

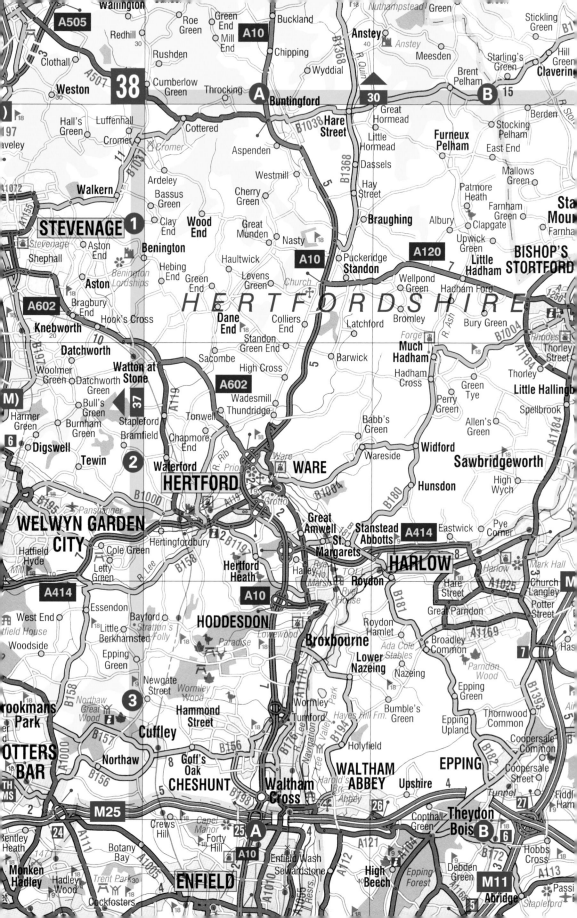

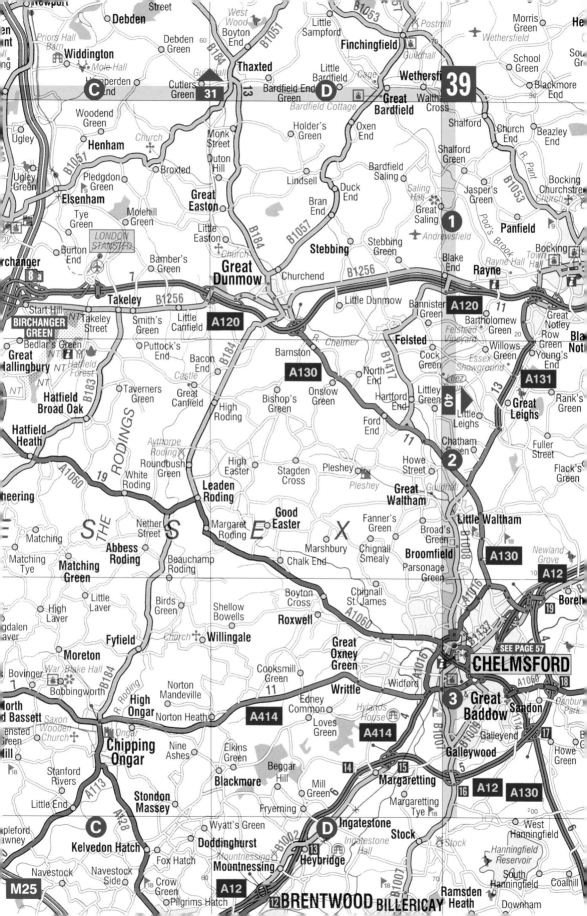

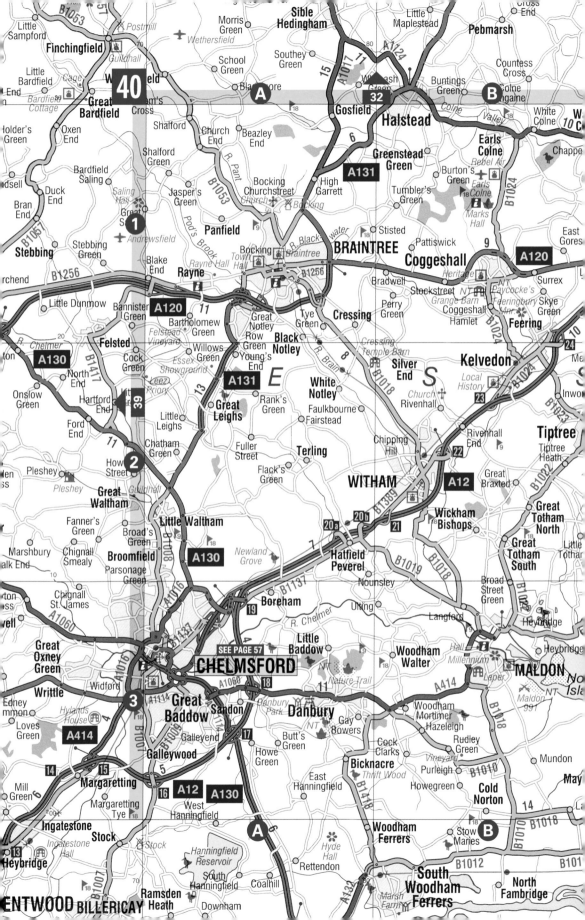

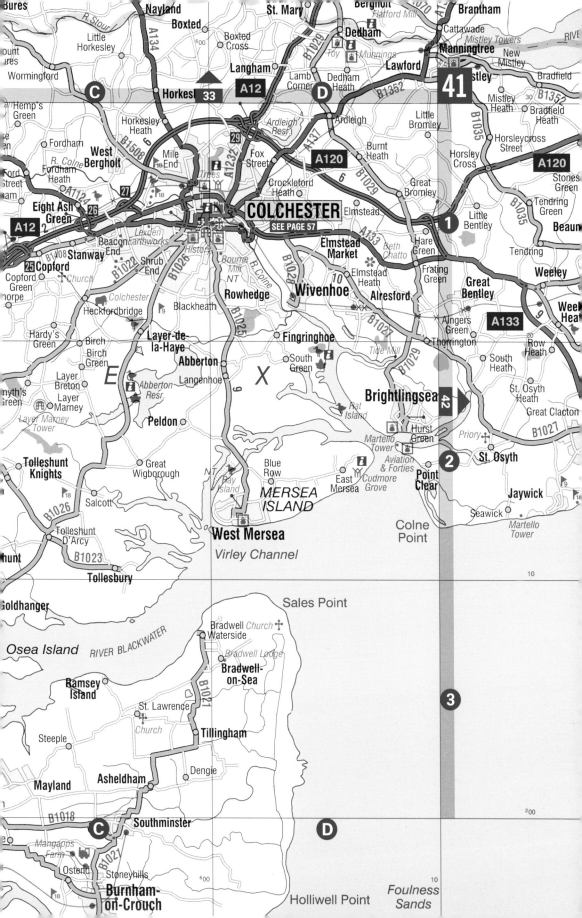

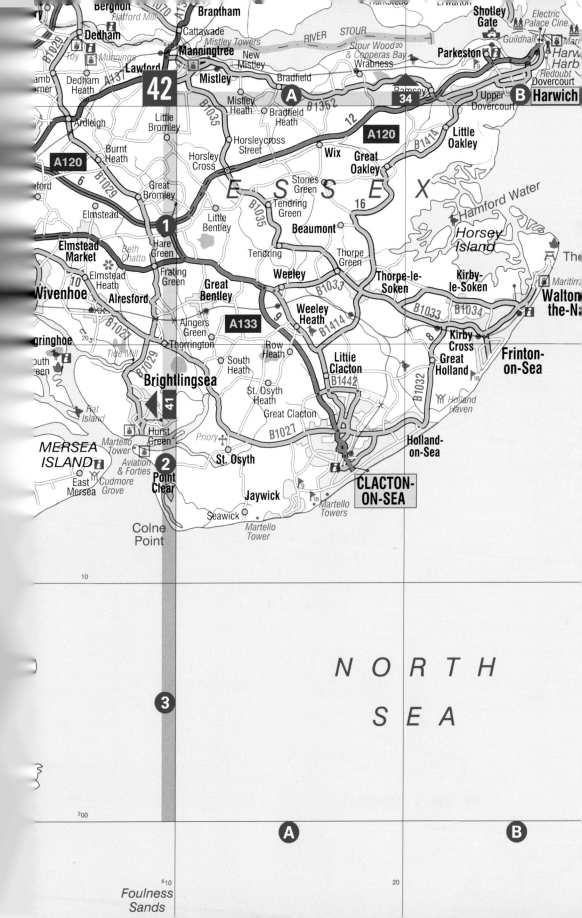

(1) A strict alphabetical order is used e.g. Abbotsley follows Abbots Langley but precedes Abbots Ripton.

(2) The map reference given refers to the actual map square in which the town spot or built-up area is located and not to the place name.

(3) Where two places of the same name occur in the same County or Unitary Authority, the nearest large town is also given; e.g. Billingford. *Norf* — 3D **9** (nr. Dereham) indicates that Billingford is located in square 3D on page **9** and is situated near Dereham in the County of Norfolk.

(4) Major towns are shown in bold, i.e. **Bedford**. *Beds* .... 2B **28** & **56**. Where they appear on a Town Plan a second page reference is given.

COUNTIES AND UNITARY AUTHORITIES with the abbreviations used in this index.

Bedfordshire : *Beds*	Greater London : *G Lon*	Luton : *Lutn*	Nottinghamshire : *Notts*
Buckinghamshire : *Buck*	Hertfordshire : *Herts*	Milton Keynes : *Mil*	Peterborough : *Pet*
Cambridgeshire : *Cambs*	Leicestershire : *Leics*	Norfolk : *Norf*	Rutland : *Rut*
Essex : *Essx*	Lincolnshire : *Linc*	Northamptonshire : *Nptn*	Suffolk : *Suff*

A

Abberton. *Essx* 2D 41
Abbess Roding. *Essx* 2C 39
Abbots Langley. *Herts* 3B 36
Abbotsley. *Cambs* 1D 29
Abbots Ripton. *Cambs* 2D 21
Abington Pigotts.
    Cambs 2A 30
Abridge. *Essx* 3B 38
Achurch. *Nptn* 1B 20
Acle. *Norf* 1D 19
Acton. *Suff* 2B 32
Ailsworth. *Pet* 3C 13
Aingers Green. *Essx* 1A 42
Aisby. *Linc* 2B 4
Akenham. *Suff* 2A 34
Alburgh. *Norf* 1B 26
Albury. *Herts* 1B 38
Alby Hill. *Norf* 2A 10
Alconbury. *Cambs* 2C 21
Alconbury Weston.
    Cambs 2C 21
Aldborough. *Norf* 2A 10
Aldbury. *Herts* 2A 36
Aldeburgh. *Suff* 1D 35
Aldeby. *Norf* 3D 19
Aldenham. *Herts* 3C 37
Alderford. *Norf* 1A 18
Alderton. *Suff* 2C 35
Aldgate. *Rut* 2A 12
Aldham. *Essx* 1C 41
Aldham. *Suff* 2D 33
Aldreth. *Cambs* 2B 22
Aldringham. *Suff* 3D 27
Aldwincle. *Nptn* 1B 20
Aley Green. *Beds* 2B 36
Algarkirk. *Linc* 2D 5
Allen's Green. *Herts* 2B 38
Allington. *Linc* 1A 4
All Saints South Elmham.
    Suff 1C 27
Alphamstone. *Essx* 3B 32
Alpheton. *Suff* 1B 32
Alpington. *Norf* 2B 18
Alresford. *Essx* 1D 41
Althorne. *Essx* 3C 41
Alwalton. *Cambs* 3C 13
Amber Hill. *Linc* 1D 5
Amersham. *Buck* 3A 36
Ampthill. *Beds* 3B 28
Ampton. *Suff* 2B 24
Amwell. *Herts* 2C 37
Ancaster. *Linc* 1A 4
Anmer. *Norf* 3A 8
Anstey. *Herts* 3B 30
Antingham. *Norf* 2B 10
Anton's Gowt. *Linc* 1D 5
Anwick. *Linc* 1C 5
Apethorpe. *Nptn* 3B 12
Apsley End. *Beds* 3C 29
Ardeley. *Herts* 1A 38
Ardleigh. *Essx* 1D 41

Arkesden. *Essx* 3B 30
Arlesey. *Beds* 3C 29
Arminghall. *Norf* 2B 18
Arms, The. *Norf* 3B 16
Armston. *Nptn* 1B 20
Arrington. *Cambs* 1A 30
Asgarby. *Linc* 1C 5
Ashbocking. *Suff* 1A 34
Ashby St Mary. *Norf* 2C 19
Ashdon. *Essx* 2C 31
Asheldham. *Essx* 3C 41
Ashen. *Essx* 2A 32
Ashfield. *Suff* 3B 26
Ashfield Green. *Suff* 2B 26
Ashill. *Norf* 2B 16
Ashley. *Cambs* 3D 23
Ashley Green. *Buck* 3A 36
Ashmanhaugh. *Norf* 3C 11
Ash Street. *Suff* 2D 33
Ashton. *Nptn* 1B 20
Ashton. *Pet* 2C 13
Ashwell. *Herts* 3D 29
Ashwell. *Rut* 1A 12
Ashwellthorpe. *Norf* 3A 18
Ashwicken. *Norf* 1A 16
Aslackby. *Linc* 2B 4
Aslacton. *Norf* 3A 18
Aspenden. *Herts* 1A 38
Asperton. *Linc* 2D 5
Aspley Guise. *Beds* 3A 28
Aspley Heath. *Beds* 3A 28
Assington. *Suff* 3C 33
Assington Green. *Suff* 1A 32
Aston. *Herts* 1D 37
Aston Abbotts. *Buck* 1A 36
Aston Clinton. *Buck* 2A 36
Aston End. *Herts* 1D 37
Astwick. *Beds* 3D 29
Astwood. *Mil* 2A 28
Aswarby. *Linc* 2B 4
Athelington. *Suff* 2B 26
Attleborough. *Norf* 3D 17
Attlebridge. *Norf* 1A 18
Audley End. *Essx* 3C 31
Aunby. *Linc* 1B 12
Aunsby. *Linc* 2B 4
Aylesbury. *Buck* 2A 36
Aylmerton. *Norf* 2A 10
Aylsham. *Norf* 3A 10
Ayot Green. *Herts* 2D 37
Ayot St Lawrence.
    Herts 2C 37
Ayot St Peter. *Herts* 2D 37
Ayston. *Rut* 2A 12

B

Babb's Green. *Herts* 2A 38
Babingley. *Norf* 3D 7
Babraham. *Cambs* 1C 31
Back Street. *Suff* 1A 32
Bacon End. *Essx* 2D 39
Baconsthorpe. *Norf* 2A 10

Bacton. *Norf* 2C 11
Bacton. *Suff* 3D 25
Bacton Green. *Norf* 2C 11
Badingham. *Suff* 3C 27
Badwell Ash. *Suff* 3C 25
Bagthorpe. *Norf* 2A 8
Bainton. *Pet* 2B 12
Baldock. *Herts* 3D 29
Bale. *Norf* 2D 9
Ballingdon. *Suff* 2B 32
Ballinger Common.
    Buck 3A 36
Balsham. *Cambs* 1C 31
Bamber's Green. *Essx* . . . 1C 39
Bangrove. *Suff* 2C 25
Banham. *Norf* 1D 25
Banningham. *Norf* 3B 10
Bannister Green. *Essx* . . . 1D 39
Banyard's Green. *Suff* . . . 2C 27
Bardfield End Green.
    Essx 3D 31
Bardfield Saling. *Essx* . . . 1D 39
Bardwell. *Suff* 2C 25
Barford. *Norf* 2A 18
Barham. *Cambs* 2C 21
Barham. *Suff* 1A 34
Bar Hill. *Cambs* 3A 22
Barholm. *Linc* 1B 12
Barking. *Suff* 1D 33
Barking Tye. *Suff* 1D 33
Barkston. *Linc* 1A 4
Barkway. *Herts* 3A 30
Barley. *Herts* 3A 30
Barleythorpe. *Rut* 2A 12
Barmer. *Norf* 2B 8
Barnack. *Pet* 2B 12
Barnardiston. *Suff* 2A 32
Barnby. *Suff* 1D 27
Barnby in the Willows.
    Notts 1A 4
Barney. *Norf* 2C 9
Barnham. *Suff* 2B 24
Barnham Broom. *Norf* 2D 17
Barningham. *Suff* 2C 25
Barnston. *Essx* 2D 39
Barnwell. *Cambs* 1B 30
Barnwell All Saints.
    Nptn 1B 20
Barnwell St Andrew.
    Nptn 1B 20
Barrington. *Cambs* 2A 30
Barrow. *Rut* 1A 12
Barrow. *Suff* 3A 24
Barroway Drove. *Norf* 2C 15
Barrowby. *Linc* 2A 4
Barrowden. *Rut* 2A 12
Barsham. *Suff* 1C 27
Bartholomew Green.
    Essx 1A 40
Bartlow. *Cambs* 2C 31
Barton. *Cambs* 1B 30
Barton Bendish. *Norf* 2A 16
Barton-le-Clay. *Beds* 3B 28
Barton Mills. *Suff* 2A 24

Barton Seagrave. *Nptn* . . . 2A 20
Barton Turf. *Norf* 3C 11
Barway. *Cambs* 2C 23
Barwick. *Herts* 2A 38
Bassingbourn. *Cambs* . . . 2A 30
Bassingthorpe. *Linc* 3A 4
Bassus Green. *Herts* 1A 38
Baston. *Linc* 1C 13
Bastwick. *Norf* 1D 19
Battisford. *Suff* 1D 33
Battisford Tye. *Suff* 1D 33
Battlesden. *Beds* 1A 36
Battlesea Green. *Suff* 2B 26
Bawburgh. *Norf* 2A 18
Bawdeswell. *Norf* 3D 9
Bawdsey. *Suff* 2C 35
Bawdsey Manor. *Suff* 3C 35
Bawsey. *Norf* 1D 15
Baxter's Green. *Suff* 1A 32
Bayford. *Herts* 3A 38
Baylham. *Suff* 1A 34
Baythorn End. *Essx* 2A 32
Baythorpe. *Linc* 1D 5
Beachamwell. *Norf* 2A 16
Beacon End. *Essx* 1C 41
Beamond End. *Buck* 3A 36
Beauchamp Roding.
    Essx 3C 39
Beaumont. *Essx* 1A 42
Beazley End. *Essx* 1A 40
Beccles. *Suff* 1D 27
Beckett End. *Norf* 3A 16
Beckingham. *Linc* 1A 4
Beck Row. *Suff* 2D 23
Bedfield. *Suff* 3B 26
Bedford. *Beds* . . . . . 2B **28** & **56**
Bedingfield. *Suff* 3A 26
Bedingham Green.
    Norf 3B 18
Bedlar's Green. *Essx* 2C 39
Bedmond. *Herts* 3B 36
Beeston. *Beds* 2C 29
Beeston. *Norf* 1C 17
Beeston Regis. *Norf* 1A 10
Beetley. *Norf* 1C 17
Begdale. *Cambs* 2B 14
Beggar Hill. *Essx* 3D 39
Beighton. *Norf* 2C 19
Belaugh. *Norf* 1B 18
Belchamp Otten. *Essx* . . . 2B 32
Belchamp St Paul.
    Essx 2A 32
Belchamp Walter. *Essx* . . . 2B 32
Bellingdon. *Buck* 3A 36
Bellmount. *Norf* 3C 7
Bell's Cross. *Suff* 1A 34
Belmesthorpe. *Rut* 1B 12
Belnie. *Linc* 2D 5
Belsize. *Herts* 3B 36
Belstead. *Suff* 2A 34
Belton. *Linc* 2A 4
Belton. *Norf* 2D 19
Benacre. *Suff* 1D 27
Bendish. *Herts* 1C 37

Bengate. *Norf* 3C **11**
Benhall Green. *Suff* 3C **27**
Benington. *Herts* 1D **37**
Benington. *Linc* 1A **6**
Benington Sea End. *Linc* 1B **6**
Bentley. *Suff* 3A **34**
Bentley Heath. *Herts* 3D **37**
Benwick. *Cambs* 3A **14**
Berden. *Essx* 1B **38**
Bergh Apton. *Norf* 2C **19**
Berkhamsted. *Herts* 3A **36**
Bessingham. *Norf* 2A **10**
Besthorpe. *Norf* 3D **17**
Bexfield. *Norf* 3D **9**
Bexwell. *Norf* 2D **15**
Beyton. *Suff* 3C **25**
Beyton Green. *Suff* 3C **25**
Bicker. *Linc* 2D **5**
Bicker Bar. *Linc* 2D **5**
Bicker Gauntlet. *Linc* 2D **5**
Bicknacre. *Essx* 3A **40**
Biddenham. *Beds* 2B **28**
Biggleswade. *Beds* 2C **29**
Bildeston. *Suff* 2C **33**
Billericay. *Essx* 3D **39**
Billingborough. *Linc* 2C **5**
Billingford. *Norf* 3D **9**
(nr. Dereham)
Billingford. *Norf* 2A **26**
(nr. Diss)
Billington. *Beds* 1A **36**
Billockby. *Norf* 1D **19**
Binham. *Norf* 2C **9**
Bintree. *Norf* 3D **9**
Birch. *Essx* 2C **41**
Bircham Newton. *Norf* 2A **8**
Bircham Tofts. *Norf* 2A **8**
Birchanger. *Essx* 1C **39**
Birch Green. *Essx* 2C **41**
Birchmoor Green. *Beds* . . . 3A **28**
Birdbrook. *Essx* 2A **32**
Birds Green. *Essx* 3C **39**
Birkholme. *Linc* 3A **4**
Birthorpe. *Linc* 2C **5**
Bisbrooke. *Rut* 3A **12**
Bishop's Green. *Essx* 2D **39**
Bishop's Stortford.
Herts 1B **38**
Bitchfield. *Linc* 3A **4**
Bittering. *Norf* 1C **17**
Black Bank. *Cambs* 1C **23**
Black Barn. *Linc* 3B **6**
Blackborough. *Norf* 1D **15**
Blackborough End.
Norf 1D **15**
Black Car. *Norf* 3D **17**
Blackheath. *Essx* 1D **41**
Blackheath. *Suff* 2D **27**
Blackjack. *Linc* 2D **5**
Blackmore. *Essx* 3D **39**
Blackmore End. *Essx* 3A **32**
Blackmore End. *Herts* . . . 2C **37**
Black Notley. *Essx* 1A **40**
Blacksmith's Green.
Suff 3A **26**
Black Street. *Suff* 1D **27**
Blackthorpe. *Suff* 3C **25**
Blake End. *Essx* 1A **40**
Blakeney. *Norf* 1D **9**
Blatherwycke. *Nptn* 3A **12**
Blaxhall. *Suff* 1C **35**
Bletchley. *Mil* 3A **28**
Bletsoe. *Beds* 1B **28**
Blickling. *Norf* 3A **10**
Blofield. *Norf* 2C **19**
Blofield Heath. *Norf* 1C **19**
Blo' Norton. *Norf* 2D **25**
Bloxholm. *Linc* 1B **4**
Blue Row. *Essx* 2D **41**
Blundeston. *Suff* 3D **19**
Blunham. *Beds* 1C **29**

Bluntisham. *Cambs* 2A **22**
Blyford. *Suff* 2D **27**
Blythburgh. *Suff* 2D **27**
Bobbingworth. *Essx* 3C **39**
Bocking. *Essx* 1A **40**
Bocking Churchstreet.
Essx 1A **40**
Bodham. *Norf* 1A **10**
Bodney. *Norf* 3B **16**
Bolnhurst. *Beds* 1B **28**
Boothby Pagnell. *Linc* 2A **4**
Booton. *Norf* 3A **10**
Boreham. *Essx* 3A **40**
Borehamwood. *Herts* . . . 3C **37**
Borley. *Essx* 2B **32**
Borley Green. *Essx* 2B **32**
Borley Green. *Suff* 3C **25**
Boston. *Linc* 1A **6**
Botany Bay. *G Lon* 3D **37**
Botesdale. *Suff* 2D **25**
Botley. *Buck* 3A **36**
Bottisham. *Cambs* 3C **23**
Boughton. *Norf* 2D **15**
Bourn. *Cambs* 1A **30**
Bourne. *Linc* 3B **4**
Bourne End. *Beds* 2A **28**
(nr. Cranfield)
Bourne End. *Beds* 3B **28**
(nr. Sharnbrook)
Bourne End. *Herts* 3B **36**
Bovingdon. *Herts* 3B **36**
Bovinger. *Essx* 3C **39**
Bow Brickhill. *Mil* 3A **28**
Bowthorpe. *Norf* 2A **18**
Box End. *Beds* 2B **28**
Boxford. *Suff* 2C **33**
Boxted. *Essx* 3C **33**
Boxted. *Suff* 1B **32**
Boxted Cross. *Essx* 3D **33**
Boxworth. *Cambs* 3A **22**
Boxworth End. *Cambs* . . . 3A **22**
Boyden End. *Suff* 1A **32**
Boyton. *Suff* 2C **35**
Boyton Cross. *Essx* 3D **39**
Boyton End. *Essx* 3D **31**
Boyton End. *Suff* 2A **32**
Bozeat. *Nptn* 1A **28**
Brabling Green. *Suff* 3B **26**
Braceborough. *Linc* 1B **12**
Braceby. *Linc* 2B **4**
Bracon Ash. *Norf* 3A **18**
Bradenham. *Norf* 2C **17**
Bradfield. *Essx* 3A **34**
Bradfield. *Norf* 2B **10**
Bradfield Combust.
Suff 1B **32**
Bradfield Heath. *Essx* 1A **42**
Bradfield St Clare. *Suff* . . . 1C **33**
Bradfield St George.
Suff 3C **25**
Bradwell. *Essx* 1B **40**
Bradwell. *Norf* 2D **19**
Bradwell-on-Sea. *Essx* . . . 3D **41**
Bradwell Waterside.
Essx 3C **41**
Bragbury End. *Herts* 1D **37**
Braintree. *Essx* 1A **40**
Braiseworth. *Suff* 2A **26**
Brakefield Green. *Norf* . . . 2D **17**
Bramerton. *Norf* 2B **18**
Bramfield. *Herts* 2D **37**
Bramfield. *Suff* 2C **27**
Bramford. *Suff* 2A **34**
Brampton. *Cambs* 2D **21**
Brampton. *Norf* 3B **10**
Brampton. *Suff* 1D **27**
Brancaster. *Norf* 1A **8**
Brancaster Staithe. *Norf* . . . 1A **8**
Brand End. *Linc* 1A **6**
Brandeston. *Suff* 3B **26**
Brandiston. *Norf* 3A **10**

Brandon. *Linc* 1A **4**
Brandon. *Suff* 1A **24**
Brandon Bank. *Cambs* . . . 1D **23**
Brandon Creek. *Norf* 3D **15**
Brandon Parva. *Norf* 2D **17**
Bran End. *Essx* 1D **39**
Brantham. *Suff* 3A **34**
Braughing. *Herts* 1A **38**
Breachwood Green.
Herts 1C **37**
Breckles. *Norf* 3C **17**
Bredfield. *Suff* 1B **34**
Brent Eleigh. *Suff* 2C **33**
Brent Pelham. *Herts* 3B **30**
Brentwood. *Essx* 3D **39**
Bressingham. *Norf* 1D **25**
Brettenham. *Norf* 1C **25**
Brettenham. *Suff* 1C **33**
Bretton. *Pet* 2C **13**
Bricket Wood. *Herts* 3C **37**
Bridge End. *Beds* 1B **28**
Bridge End. *Linc* 2C **5**
Bridge Green. *Essx* 3B **30**
Bridge Street. *Suff* 2B **32**
Bridgham. *Norf* 1C **25**
Briggate. *Norf* 3C **11**
Brightlingsea. *Essx* 2D **41**
Brightwell. *Suff* 2B **34**
Brigstock. *Nptn* 1A **20**
Bringhurst. *Leics* 3A **12**
Brington. *Cambs* 2B **20**
Briningham. *Norf* 2D **9**
Brinkley. *Cambs* 1D **31**
Brinton. *Norf* 2D **9**
Brisley. *Norf* 3C **9**
Briston. *Norf* 2D **9**
Broad Green. *Beds* 2A **28**
Broad Green. *Cambs* 1D **31**
Broad Hill. *Cambs* 2C **23**
Broadley Common.
Essx 3B **38**
Broad's Green. *Essx* 2D **39**
Broad Street Green.
Essx 3B **40**
Broadway. *Suff* 2C **27**
Brockdish. *Norf* 2B **26**
Brockford Street. *Suff* 3A **26**
Brockley. *Suff* 2B **24**
Brockley Green. *Suff* 2A **32**
(nr. Bury St Edmunds)
Brockley Green. *Suff* 1B **32**
(nr. Haverhill)
Brogborough. *Beds* 3A **28**
Brome. *Suff* 2A **26**
Brome Street. *Suff* 2A **26**
Bromeswell. *Suff* 1C **35**
Bromham. *Beds* 1B **28**
Bromley. *Herts* 1B **38**
Brooke. *Norf* 3B **18**
Brooke. *Rut* 2A **12**
Brookmans Park. *Herts* . . . 3D **37**
Brookville. *Norf* 3A **16**
Broom. *Beds* 2C **29**
Broome. *Norf* 3C **19**
Broomfield. *Essx* 2A **40**
Broom Green. *Norf* 3C **9**
Broomhill. *Norf* 2D **15**
Broomholm. *Norf* 2C **11**
Brotherhouse Bar. *Linc* . . . 1D **13**
Brothertoft. *Linc* 1D **5**
Broughton. *Cambs* 2D **21**
Broughton. *Mil* 3A **28**
Browston Green. *Norf* 2D **19**
Broxbourne. *Herts* 3A **38**
Broxted. *Essx* 1C **39**
Bruisyard. *Suff* 3C **27**
Bruisyard Street. *Suff* 3C **27**
Brundall. *Norf* 2C **19**
Brundish. *Norf* 3C **19**
Brundish. *Suff* 3B **26**
Brundish Street. *Suff* 2B **26**

Bryant's Bottom. *Buck* . . . 3A **36**
Buckden. *Cambs* 3C **21**
Buckenham. *Norf* 2C **19**
Buckland. *Buck* 2A **36**
Buckland. *Herts* 3A **30**
Buckland Common.
Buck 3A **36**
Bucklegate. *Linc* 2A **6**
Bucklesham. *Suff* 2B **34**
Buckminster. *Leics* 3A **4**
Bucks Hill. *Herts* 3B **36**
Buckworth. *Cambs* 2C **21**
Bulbourne. *Herts* 2A **36**
Bulby. *Linc* 3B **4**
Bull's Green. *Herts* 2D **37**
Bulmer. *Essx* 2B **32**
Bulmer Tye. *Essx* 3B **32**
Bulwick. *Nptn* 3A **12**
Bumble's Green. *Essx* 3B **38**
Bungay. *Suff* 1C **27**
Bunker's Hill. *Cambs* 2B **14**
Bunker's Hill. *Suff* 2D **19**
Buntingford. *Herts* 1A **38**
Buntings Green. *Essx* 3B **32**
Bunwell. *Norf* 3A **18**
Burcott. *Buck* 1A **36**
Bures. *Suff* 3C **33**
Burgate Great Green.
Suff 2D **25**
Burgate Little Green.
Suff 2D **25**
Burgh. *Suff* 1B **34**
Burgh Castle. *Norf* 2D **19**
Burgh next Aylsham.
Norf 3B **10**
Burgh St Margaret.
Norf 1D **19**
Burgh St Peter. *Norf* 3D **19**
Burley. *Rut* 1A **12**
Burnham Deepdale. *Norf* . . . 1B **8**
Burnham Green. *Herts* . . . 2D **37**
Burnham Market. *Norf* 1B **8**
Burnham Norton. *Norf* 1B **8**
Burnham-on-Crouch.
Essx 3C **41**
Burnham Overy Staithe.
Norf 1B **8**
Burnham Overy Town.
Norf 1B **8**
Burnham Thorpe. *Norf* 1B **8**
Burnt Heath. *Essx* 1D **41**
Burntstalk. *Norf* 2A **8**
Burrough End. *Cambs* 1D **31**
Burrough Green. *Cambs* . . . 1D **31**
Burstall. *Suff* 2D **33**
Burston. *Norf* 1A **26**
Burthorpe. *Suff* 3A **24**
Burtoft. *Linc* 2D **5**
Burton Coggles. *Linc* 3A **4**
Burton Corner. *Linc* 1A **6**
Burton End. *Cambs* 2D **31**
Burton End. *Essx* 1C **39**
Burton Latimer. *Nptn* 2A **20**
Burton Pedwardine. *Linc* . . . 1C **5**
Burton's Green. *Essx* 1B **40**
Burwell. *Cambs* 3C **23**
Bury. *Cambs* 1D **21**
Bury Green. *Herts* 1B **38**
Bury St Edmunds.
Suff . . . . 3B **24 & 56**
Bush Green. *Norf* 3D **17**
(nr. Attleborough)
Bush Green. *Norf* 1B **26**
(nr. Harleston)
Bush Green. *Suff* 1C **33**
Bushmead. *Beds* 3C **21**
Bushy Common. *Norf* 1C **17**
Bustard Green. *Essx* 1D **39**
Butley. *Suff* 1C **35**
Butley High Corner.
Suff 2C **35**

Butterwick. *Linc* 1A **6**
Butt's Green. *Essx* 3A **40**
Buxhall. *Suff* 1D **33**
Buxton. *Norf* 3B **10**
Bygrave. *Herts* 3D **29**
Bythorn. *Cambs* 2B **20**

C

Caddington. *Beds* 2B **36**
Cadwell. *Herts* 3C **29**
Caister-on-Sea. *Norf* 1D **19**
Caister St Edmund.
    Norf 2B **18**
Cake Street. *Suff* 2D **23**
Calais Street. *Suff* 2C **33**
Caldecote. *Cambs* 1A **30**
    (nr. Cambridge)
Caldecote. *Cambs* 1C **21**
    (nr. Peterborough)
Caldecote. *Herts* 3D **29**
Caldecott. *Nptn* 3A **20**
Caldecott. *Rut* 3A **12**
Calford Green. *Suff* 2D **31**
California. *Norf* 1D **19**
California. *Suff* 2A **34**
Calthorpe. *Norf* 2A **10**
Calthorpe Street. *Norf* 3D **11**
Cambourne. *Cambs* 1A **30**
Cambridge.
    Cambs . . . . .1B **30** & **57**
Cambridge City Airport.
    Cambs 1B **30**
Campsea Ashe. *Suff* 1C **35**
Camps End. *Cambs* 2D **31**
Campton. *Beds* 3C **29**
Candle Street. *Suff* 2D **25**
Cangate. *Norf* 3C **11**
Canham's Green. *Suff* 3D **25**
Cantley. *Norf* 2C **19**
Capel Green. *Suff* 2C **35**
Capel St Andrew. *Suff* 2C **35**
Capel St Mary. *Suff* 3D **33**
Carbrooke. *Norf* 2C **17**
Cardinal's Green.
    Cambs 2D **31**
Cardington. *Beds* 2B **28**
Careby. *Linc* 1B **12**
Cargate Green. *Norf* 1C **19**
Carlby. *Linc* 1B **12**
Carleton Forehoe. *Norf* . . .2D **17**
Carleton Rode. *Norf* 3A **18**
Carleton St Peter. *Norf* . . .2C **19**
Carlton. *Beds* 1A **28**
Carlton. *Cambs* 1D **31**
Carlton. *Suff* 3C **27**
Carlton Colville. *Suff* 3D **19**
Carlton Scroop. *Linc* 1A **4**
Castle Acre. *Norf* 1B **16**
Castle Ashby. *Nptn* 1A **28**
Castle Bytham. *Linc* 1A **12**
Castle Camps. *Cambs* 2D **31**
Castle Hedingham. *Essx.* . .3A **32**
Castle Hill. *Suff* 2A **34**
Castle Rising. *Norf* 3D **7**
Caston. *Norf* 3C **17**
Castor. *Pet* 3C **13**
Catfield. *Norf* 3C **11**
Catfield Common. *Norf* . . .3C **11**
Cattawade. *Suff* 3A **34**
Catton. *Norf* 1B **18**
Catworth. *Cambs* 2B **20**
Cavendish. *Suff* 2B **32**
Cavenham. *Suff* 3A **24**
Cawston. *Norf* 3A **10**
Cawthorpe. *Linc* 3B **4**
Caxton. *Cambs* 1A **30**
Caythorpe. *Linc* 1A **4**
Cess. *Norf* 1D **19**
Chadstone. *Nptn* 1A **28**

Chainbridge. *Cambs* 2B **14**
Chain Bridge. *Linc* 1A **6**
Chalk End. *Essx* 2D **39**
Chalton. *Beds* 1C **29**
    (nr. Bedford)
Chalton. *Beds* 1B **36**
    (nr. Luton)
Chandler's Cross. *Herts* . . .3B **36**
Channel End. *Beds* 1C **29**
Chantry. *Suff* 2A **34**
Chapelbridge. *Cambs* 3D **13**
Chapel End. *Beds* 2B **28**
Chapelgate. *Linc* 3B **6**
Chapmore End. *Herts* 2A **38**
Chappel. *Essx* 1B **40**
Charles Tye. *Suff* 1D **33**
Charlton. *Herts* 1C **37**
Charsfield. *Suff* 1B **34**
Chartridge. *Buck* 3A **36**
Chatham Green. *Essx* 2A **40**
Chatteris. *Cambs* 1A **22**
Chattisham. *Suff* 2D **33**
Chaulden. *Herts* 3A **36**
Chawston. *Beds* 1C **29**
Chedburgh. *Suff* 1A **32**
Cheddington. *Buck* 2A **36**
Chedgrave. *Norf* 3C **19**
Chediston. *Suff* 2C **27**
Chediston Green. *Suff* 2C **27**
Chellington. *Beds* 1A **28**
Chelmondiston. *Suff* 3B **34**
Chelmsford. *Essx* . .3A **40** & **57**
Chelsworth. *Suff* 2C **33**
Chelveston. *Nptn* 3A **20**
Chenies. *Buck* 3B **36**
Chequers Corner. *Norf* . . .2B **14**
Cherry Green. *Herts* 1A **38**
Cherry Hinton. *Cambs* 1B **30**
Chesham. *Buck* 3A **36**
Chesham Bois. *Buck* 3A **36**
Cheshunt. *Herts* 3A **38**
Chesterton. *Cambs* 3B **22**
    (nr. Cambridge)
Chesterton. *Cambs* 3C **13**
    (nr. Peterborough)
Chettisham. *Cambs* 1C **23**
Cheveley. *Cambs* 3D **23**
Chevington. *Suff* 1A **32**
Chicheley. *Mil* 2A **28**
Chickering. *Suff* 2B **26**
Chignall St James.
    Essx 3D **39**
Chignall Smealy. *Essx* 2D **39**
Childwick Green. *Herts* . . .2C **37**
Chillesford. *Suff* 1C **35**
Chiltern Green. *Beds* 2C **37**
Chilton Street. *Suff* 2A **32**
Chimney Street. *Suff* 2A **32**
Chippenham. *Cambs* 3D **23**
Chipperfield. *Herts* 3B **36**
Chipping. *Herts* 3A **30**
Chipping Hill. *Essx* 2B **40**
Chipping Ongar. *Essx* 3C **39**
Chiswell Green. *Herts* 3C **37**
Chittering. *Cambs* 3A **22**
Cholesbury. *Buck* 3A **36**
Chrishall. *Essx* 3B **30**
Christchurch. *Cambs* 3B **14**
Church End. *Beds* 1A **36**
    (nr. Dunstable)
Church End. *Beds* 3C **29**
    (nr. Stotfold)
Church End. *Beds* 2A **28**
    (nr. Woburn)
Church End. *Cambs* 1B **30**
    (nr. Cambridge)
Church End. *Cambs* 1D **21**
    (nr. Sawtry)
Church End. *Cambs* 2A **22**
    (nr. Willingham)

Church End. *Cambs* 2A **14**
    (nr. Wisbech)
Church End. *Essx* 1A **40**
    (nr. Braintree)
Churchend. *Essx* 1D **39**
    (nr. Great Dunmow)
Church End. *Essx* 2C **31**
    (nr. Saffron Walden)
Church End. *Linc* 2D **5**
Church End. *Norf* 1C **15**
Church Langley. *Essx* 3B **38**
Church Street. *Suff* 1D **27**
Clacton-on-Sea. *Essx* . . .2A **42**
Clapgate. *Herts* 1B **38**
Clapham. *Beds* 1B **28**
Clare. *Suff* 2A **32**
Clark's Hill. *Linc* 3A **6**
Clavering. *Essx* 3B **30**
Claxton. *Norf* 2C **19**
Clay Common. *Suff* 1D **27**
Claydon. *Suff* 1A **34**
Clay End. *Herts* 1A **38**
Clayhythe. *Cambs* 3C **23**
Clay Lake. *Linc* 3D **5**
Claypole. *Linc* 1A **4**
Clenchwarton. *Norf* 3C **7**
Cley next the Sea. *Norf* . . .1D **9**
Clifton. *Beds* 3C **29**
Clifton Reynes. *Mil* 1A **28**
Cliftonville. *Norf* 2C **11**
Clint Green. *Norf* 1D **17**
Clippesby. *Norf* 1D **19**
Clippings Green. *Norf* 1D **17**
Clipsham. *Rut* 1A **12**
Clophill. *Beds* 3B **28**
Clopton. *Nptn* 1B **20**
Clopton Corner. *Suff* 1B **34**
Clopton Green. *Suff* 1A **32**
Clothall. *Herts* 3D **29**
Coalhill. *Essx* 3A **40**
Coates. *Cambs* 3A **14**
Cockayne Hatley. *Beds* . . .2D **29**
Cock Clarks. *Essx* 3B **40**
Cockernhoe. *Herts* 1C **37**
Cockfield. *Suff* 1C **33**
Cockfosters. *G Lon* 3D **37**
Cock Green. *Essx* 2D **39**
Cockley Cley. *Norf* 2A **16**
Cockthorpe. *Norf* 1C **9**
Coddenham. *Suff* 1A **34**
Coddenham Green.
    Suff 1A **34**
Codicote. *Herts* 2D **37**
Coggeshall. *Essx* 1B **40**
Coggeshall Hamlet.
    Essx 1B **40**
Colby. *Norf* 2B **10**
Colchester. *Essx* . . .1D **41** & **57**
Cold Brayfield. *Mil* 1A **28**
Coldfair Green. *Suff* 3D **27**
Coldham. *Cambs* 2B **14**
Cold Norton. *Essx* 3B **40**
Colegate End. *Norf* 1A **26**
Cole Green. *Herts* 2D **37**
Coleman Green. *Herts* 2C **37**
Colesden. *Beds* 1C **29**
Colkirk. *Norf* 3C **9**
Colliers End. *Herts* 1A **38**
Collyweston. *Nptn* 2A **12**
Colmworth. *Beds* 1C **29**
Colne. *Cambs* 2A **22**
Colne Engaine. *Essx* 3B **32**
Colney. *Norf* 2A **18**
Colney Heath. *Herts* 3D **37**
Colney Street. *Herts* 3C **37**
Colsterworth. *Linc* 3A **4**
Coltishall. *Norf* 1B **18**
Colton. *Norf* 2A **18**
Comberton. *Cambs* 1A **30**
Combs. *Suff* 1D **33**
Combs Ford. *Suff* 1D **33**

Commercial End.
    Cambs 3C **23**
Coney Weston. *Suff* 2C **25**
Congham. *Norf* 3A **8**
Conington. *Cambs* 3A **22**
    (nr. Fenstanton)
Conington. *Cambs* 1C **21**
    (nr. Sawtry)
Conyers Green. *Suff* 3B **24**
Cookley. *Suff* 2C **27**
Cooksmill Green. *Essx* 3D **39**
Coopersale Common.
    Essx 3B **38**
Coopersale Street.
    Essx 3B **38**
Copalder Corner.
    Cambs 3A **14**
Copdock. *Suff* 2A **34**
Copford. *Essx* 1C **41**
Copford Green. *Essx* 1C **41**
Cople. *Beds* 2C **29**
Coppingford. *Cambs* 1C **21**
Copthall Green. *Essx* 3B **38**
Copy's Green. *Norf* 2C **9**
Corby. *Nptn* 1A **20**
Corby Glen. *Linc* 3B **4**
Cornish Hall End. *Essx* 3D **31**
Corpusty. *Norf* 3A **10**
Corton. *Suff* 3D **19**
Costessey. *Norf* 1A **18**
Coston. *Leics* 3A **4**
Coston. *Norf* 2D **17**
Coton. *Cambs* 1B **30**
Cottenham. *Cambs* 3B **22**
Cottered. *Herts* 1A **38**
Cotterstock. *Nptn* 3B **12**
Cottesmore. *Rut* 1A **12**
Cottingham. *Nptn* 3A **12**
Cotton. *Suff* 3D **25**
Cotton End. *Beds* 2B **28**
Countess Cross. *Essx* 3B **32**
Covehithe. *Suff* 1D **27**
Coveney. *Cambs* 1B **22**
Covington. *Cambs* 2B **20**
Cowbit. *Linc* 1D **13**
Cowlinge. *Suff* 1A **32**
Cox Common. *Suff* 1D **27**
Coxford. *Norf* 3B **8**
Crabgate. *Norf* 3D **9**
Crafton. *Buck* 2A **36**
Crane's Corner. *Norf* 1C **17**
Cranfield. *Beds* 2A **28**
Cranford St Andrew.
    Nptn 2A **20**
Cranford St John.
    Nptn 2A **20**
Cranley. *Suff* 2A **26**
Cranmer Green. *Suff* 2D **25**
Cranmore. *Linc* 2C **13**
Cransford. *Suff* 3C **27**
Cranwell. *Linc* 1B **4**
Cranwich. *Norf* 3A **16**
Cranworth. *Norf* 2C **17**
Cratfield. *Suff* 2C **27**
Craymere Beck. *Norf* 2D **9**
Creeting St Mary. *Suff* 1D **33**
Creeting St Peter. *Suff* 1D **33**
Creeton. *Linc* 3B **4**
Cressing. *Essx* 1A **40**
Cretingham. *Suff* 3B **26**
Crews Hill. *G Lon* 3A **38**
Crimplesham. *Norf* 2D **15**
Cringleford. *Norf* 2A **18**
Crockleford Heath.
    Essx 1D **41**
Cromer. *Herts* 1D **37**
Cromer. *Norf* 1B **10**
Crossdale Street. *Norf* 2B **10**
Cross End. *Essx* 3B **32**
Cross Green. *Suff* 1B **32**
    (nr. Cockfield)

Cross Green. *Suff* 1C **33**
(nr. Hitcham)
Cross Street. *Suff* 2A **26**
Crostwick. *Norf* 1B **18**
Crostwight. *Norf* 3C **11**
Crow End. *Cambs* 1A **30**
Crowfield. *Suff* 1A **34**
Crow Green. *Essx* 3C **39**
Crowland. *Linc* 1D **13**
Crowland. *Suff* 2D **25**
Crown Corner. *Suff* 2B **26**
Crownthorpe. *Norf* 2D **17**
Crowshill. *Norf* 2C **17**
Croxton. *Cambs* 3D **21**
Croxton. *Norf* 2C **9**
(nr. Fakenham)
Croxton. *Norf* 1B **24**
(nr. Thetford)
Croydon. *Cambs* 2A **30**
Cryers Hill. *Buck* 3A **36**
Cublington. *Buck* 1A **36**
Cuckoo Bridge. *Linc* 3D **5**
Cuffley. *Herts* 3A **38**
Culford. *Suff* 3B **24**
Culverthorpe. *Linc* 1B **4**
Cumberlow Green.
Herts 3A **30**
Cutlers Green. *Essx* 3C **31**

D

Daffy Green. *Norf* 2C **17**
Dagnall. *Buck* 2A **36**
Dalham. *Suff* 3A **24**
Dallinghoo. *Suff* 1B **34**
Damgate. *Norf* 2D **19**
(nr. Acle)
Damgate. *Norf* 1D **19**
(nr. Martham)
Dam Green. *Norf* 1D **25**
Danbury. *Essx* 3A **40**
Dane End. *Herts* 1A **38**
Darmsden. *Suff* 1D **33**
Darrow Green. *Norf* 1B **26**
Darsham. *Suff* 3D **27**
Dassels. *Herts* 1A **38**
Datchworth. *Herts* 2D **37**
Datchworth Green.
Herts 2D **37**
Dawsmere. *Linc* 2B **6**
Debach. *Suff* 1B **34**
Debden. *Essx* 3C **31**
Debden Green. *Essx* 3B **38**
(nr. Loughton)
Debden Green. *Essx* 3C **31**
(nr. Saffron Walden)
Debenham. *Suff* 3A **26**
Dedham. *Essx* 3D **33**
Dedham Heath. *Essx* 3D **33**
Deene. *Nptn* 3A **12**
Deenethorpe. *Nptn* 3A **12**
Deeping Gate. *Pet* 2C **13**
Deeping St James.
Linc 2C **13**
Deeping St Nicholas.
Linc 1D **13**
Dell, The. *Suff* 3D **19**
Dembleby. *Linc* 2B **4**
Denford. *Nptn* 2A **20**
Dengie. *Essx* 3C **41**
Denham. *Suff* 3A **24**
(nr. Bury St Edmunds)
Denham. *Suff* 2A **25**
(nr. Eye)
Denham Street. *Suff* 2A **26**
Dennington. *Suff* 3B **26**
Denny End. *Cambs* 3B **22**
Denston. *Suff* 1A **32**
Denton. *Cambs* 1C **21**

Denton. *Linc* 2A **4**
Denton. *Norf* 1B **26**
Denver. *Norf* 2D **15**
Deopham. *Norf* 2D **17**
Deopham Green. *Norf* . . . 3D **17**
Depden. *Suff* 1A **32**
Depden Green. *Suff* 1A **32**
Dereham. *Norf* 1C **17**
Dersingham. *Norf* 2D **7**
Dickleburgh. *Norf* 1A **26**
Diddington. *Cambs* 3C **21**
Digswell. *Herts* 2D **37**
Dilham. *Norf* 3C **11**
Dillington. *Cambs* 3C **21**
Diss. *Norf* 2A **26**
Ditchingham. *Norf* 3C **19**
Ditton Green. *Cambs* 1D **31**
Docking. *Norf* 2A **8**
Doddinghurst. *Essx* 3C **39**
Doddington. *Cambs* 3A **14**
Doddshill. *Norf* 2A **8**
Dogsthorpe. *Pet* 2D **13**
Donington. *Linc* 2D **5**
Donington Eaudike. *Linc* . . 2D **5**
Donington South Ing.
Linc 2D **5**
Dorking Tye. *Suff* 3C **33**
Dorrington. *Linc* 1B **4**
Dovercourt. *Essx* 3B **34**
Downfield. *Cambs* 2D **23**
Downham. *Essx* 3A **40**
Downham Market.
Norf 2D **15**
Dowsby. *Linc* 3C **5**
Dowsdale. *Linc* 1D **13**
Drabblegate. *Norf* 3B **10**
Drayton. *Linc* 2D **5**
Drayton. *Norf* 1A **18**
Drayton Beauchamp.
Buck 2A **36**
Drayton Parslow. *Buck* . . 1A **36**
Drinkstone. *Suff* 3C **25**
Drinkstone Green. *Suff* . . 3C **25**
Drury Square. *Norf* 1C **17**
Dry Doddington. *Linc* 1A **4**
Dry Drayton. *Cambs* 3A **22**
Duck End. *Essx* 1D **39**
Duddenhoe End. *Essx* . . . 3B **30**
Duddington. *Nptn* 2A **12**
Dullingham. *Cambs* 1D **31**
Dullingham Ley.
Cambs 1D **31**
Duloe. *Beds* 3C **21**
Dunsby. *Linc* 3C **5**
Dunsmore. *Buck* 3A **36**
Dunstable. *Beds* 1B **36**
Dunstall Green. *Suff* 3A **24**
Dunston. *Norf* 2B **18**
Dunton. *Beds* 2D **29**
Dunton. *Norf* 2B **8**
Dunton Patch. *Norf* 2B **8**
Dunwich. *Suff* 2D **27**
Duton Hill. *Essx* 1D **39**
Duxford. *Cambs* 2B **30**
Dyke. *Linc* 3C **5**

E

Eaglethorpe. *Nptn* 3B **12**
Earith. *Cambs* 2A **22**
Earlesfield. *Linc* 2A **4**
Earlham. *Norf* 2A **18**
Earls Colne. *Essx* 1B **40**
Earl's Green. *Suff* 3D **25**
Earl Soham. *Suff* 3B **26**
Earl Stonham. *Suff* 1A **34**
Earsham. *Norf* 1C **27**
Earsham Street. *Suff* 2B **26**
East Barsham. *Norf* 2C **9**
East Beckham. *Norf* 1A **10**

East Bergholt. *Suff* 3D **33**
East Bliney. *Norf* 1C **17**
East Bridge. *Suff* 3D **27**
East Carleton. *Norf* 2A **18**
East End. *Cambs* 2A **22**
East End. *Herts* 1B **38**
East End. *Suff* 3A **34**
Eastgate. *Norf* 3A **10**
East Gores. *Essx* 1B **40**
East Hanningfield. *Essx* . . 3A **40**
East Harling. *Norf* 1C **25**
East Hatley. *Cambs* 1D **29**
Easthaugh. *Norf* 1D **17**
East Heckington. *Linc* 1C **5**
Easthorpe. *Essx* 1C **41**
East Hyde. *Beds* 2C **37**
East Lexham. *Norf* 1B **16**
East Mersea. *Essx* 2D **41**
Eastmoor. *Norf* 2A **16**
Easton. *Cambs* 2C **21**
Easton. *Linc* 3A **4**
Easton. *Norf* 1A **18**
Easton. *Suff* 1B **34**
Easton Maudit. *Nptn* 1A **28**
Easton on the Hill.
Nptn 2B **12**
East Perry. *Cambs* 3C **21**
East Raynham. *Norf* 3B **8**
Eastrea. *Cambs* 3D **13**
East Rudham. *Norf* 3B **8**
East Runton. *Norf* 1A **10**
East Ruston. *Norf* 3C **11**
East Somerton. *Norf* 1D **19**
East Tuddenham. *Norf* . . . 1D **17**
East Walton. *Norf* 1A **16**
Eastwick. *Herts* 2B **38**
East Winch. *Norf* 1D **15**
Eastwood End. *Cambs* . . 3B **14**
Eaton. *Norf* 2D **7**
(nr. Heacham)
Eaton. *Norf* 2B **18**
(nr. Norwich)
Eaton Bray. *Beds* 1A **36**
Eaton Socon. *Cambs* 1C **29**
Eau Brink. *Norf* 1C **15**
Eccles on Sea. *Norf* 3D **11**
Eccles Road. *Norf* 3D **17**
Edenham. *Linc* 3B **4**
Edgefield. *Norf* 2D **9**
Edgefield Street. *Norf* 2D **9**
Edingthorpe. *Norf* 2C **11**
Edith Weston. *Rut* 2A **12**
Edlesborough. *Buck* 2A **36**
Edmondthorpe. *Leics* 1A **12**
Edney Common. *Essx* . . . 3D **39**
Edwardstone. *Suff* 2C **33**
Edworth. *Beds* 2D **29**
Eggington. *Beds* 1A **36**
Egleton. *Rut* 2A **12**
Eight Ash Green. *Essx* . . . 1C **41**
Eldernell. *Cambs* 3A **14**
Elder Street. *Essx* 3C **31**
Elford Closes. *Cambs* . . . 2B **22**
Elkins Green. *Essx* 3D **39**
Ellenbrook. *Herts* 3D **37**
Ellingham. *Norf* 3C **19**
Ellington. *Cambs* 2C **21**
Ellington Thorpe.
Cambs 2C **21**
Ellough. *Suff* 1D **27**
Elm. *Cambs* 2B **14**
Elmdon. *Essx* 3B **30**
Elmsett. *Suff* 2D **33**
Elmstead. *Essx* 1D **41**
Elmstead Heath. *Essx* . . . 1D **41**
Elmstead Market. *Essx* . . 1D **41**
Elmswell. *Suff* 3C **25**
Elsenham. *Essx* 1C **39**
Elsing. *Norf* 1D **17**
Elsthorpe. *Linc* 3B **4**
Elstow. *Beds* 2B **28**

Elsworth. *Cambs* 3A **22**
Eltisley. *Cambs* 1D **29**
Elton. *Cambs* 3B **12**
Elveden. *Suff* 2B **24**
Ely. *Cambs* . . . . . . 1C **23** & **58**
Emberton. *Mil* 2A **28**
Emneth. *Norf* 2B **14**
Emneth Hungate. *Norf* . . . 2C **15**
Empingham. *Rut* 2A **12**
Enfield. *G Lon* 3A **38**
Enfield Wash. *G Lon* 3A **38**
Epping. *Essx* 3B **38**
Epping Green. *Essx* 3B **38**
Epping Green. *Herts* 3D **37**
Epping Upland. *Essx* 3B **38**
Eriswell. *Suff* 2A **24**
Erpingham. *Norf* 2A **10**
Erwarton. *Suff* 3B **34**
Essendine. *Rut* 1B **12**
Essendon. *Herts* 3D **37**
Etling Green. *Norf* 1D **17**
Etton. *Pet* 2C **13**
Euston. *Suff* 2B **24**
Evedon. *Linc* 1B **4**
Eversholt. *Beds* 3A **28**
Everton. *Beds* 1D **29**
Ewerby. *Linc* 1C **5**
Exning. *Suff* 3D **23**
Exton. *Rut* 1A **12**
Eye. *Pet* 2D **13**
Eye. *Suff* 2A **26**
Eye Green. *Pet* 2D **13**
Eyeworth. *Beds* 2D **29**
Eyke. *Suff* 1C **35**
Eynesbury. *Cambs* 1C **29**

F

Fair Green. *Norf* 1D **15**
Fairstead. *Essx* 2A **40**
Fairstead. *Norf* 1D **15**
Fakenham. *Norf* 3C **9**
Fakenham Magna. *Suff* . . 2C **25**
Falkenham. *Suff* 3B **34**
Fancott. *Beds* 1B **36**
Fanner's Green. *Essx* . . . 2D **39**
Farcet. *Cambs* 3D **13**
Farley Green. *Suff* 1A **32**
Farndish. *Beds* 3A **20**
Farnham. *Essx* 1B **38**
Farnham. *Suff* 3C **27**
Farnham Green. *Essx* . . . 1B **38**
Faulkbourne. *Essx* 2A **40**
Feering. *Essx* 1B **40**
Felbrigg. *Norf* 2B **10**
Felden. *Herts* 3B **36**
Felixstowe. *Suff* 3B **34**
Felixstowe Ferry. *Suff* . . . 3C **35**
Felmersham. *Beds* 1A **28**
Felmingham. *Norf* 3B **10**
Felsham. *Suff* 1C **33**
Felsted. *Essx* 1D **39**
Felthorpe. *Norf* 1A **18**
Feltwell. *Norf* 3A **16**
Fen Ditton. *Cambs* 3B **22**
Fen Drayton. *Cambs* 3A **22**
Fen End. *Linc* 3D **5**
Fenhouses. *Linc* 1D **5**
Fenny Stratford. *Mil* 3A **28**
Fenstanton. *Cambs* 3A **22**
Fen Street. *Norf* 3D **17**
Fenton. *Cambs* 2A **22**
Fenton. *Linc* 1A **4**
Ferry Hill. *Cambs* 1A **22**
Fersfield. *Norf* 1D **25**
Fiddlers Hamlet. *Essx* . . . 3B **38**
Field Dalling. *Norf* 2D **9**
Filby. *Norf* 1D **19**
Filgrave. *Mil* 2A **28**
Fincham. *Norf* 2D **15**

Finchingfield. *Essx* 3D **31**
Finedon. *Nptn* 2A **20**
Fingal Street. *Suff* 2B **26**
Fingringhoe. *Essx* 1D **41**
Finningham. *Suff* 3D **25**
Fishley. *Norf* 1D **19**
Fishtoft. *Linc* 1A **6**
Fishtoft Drove. *Linc* 1A **6**
Fitton End. *Cambs* 1B **14**
Flack's Green. *Essx* 2A **40**
Flamstead. *Herts* 2B **36**
Flaunden. *Herts* 3B **36**
Fleet. *Linc* 3A **6**
Fleet Hargate. *Linc* 3A **6**
Fleetville. *Herts* 3C **37**
Fleggburgh. *Norf* 1D **19**
Flempton. *Suff* 3B **24**
Flitcham. *Norf* 3A **8**
Flitton. *Beds* 3B **28**
Flitwick. *Beds* 3B **28**
Flixton. *Suff* 1C **27**
Flood's Ferry. *Cambs* 3A **14**
Flordon. *Norf* 3A **18**
Flowton. *Suff* 2D **33**
Folkingham. *Linc* 2B **4**
Folksworth. *Cambs* 3C **13**
Folly, The. *Herts* 2C **37**
Ford End. *Essx* 2D **39**
Fordham. *Cambs* 2D **23**
Fordham. *Essx* 1C **41**
Fordham. *Norf* 3D **15**
Fordham Heath. *Essx* 1C **41**
Ford Street. *Essx* 1C **41**
Forncett End. *Norf* 3A **18**
Forncett St Mary. *Norf* ...3A **18**
Forncett St Peter. *Norf* ...3A **18**
Fornham All Saints.
      Suff 3B **24**
Fornham St Martin.
      Suff 3B **24**
Forty Hill. *G Lon* 3A **38**
Forward Green. *Suff* 1D **33**
Fosdyke. *Linc* 2A **6**
Foster Street. *Essx* 3B **38**
Foston. *Linc* 1A **4**
Fotheringhay. *Nptn* 3B **12**
Foul Anchor. *Cambs* 1B **14**
Foulden. *Norf* 3A **16**
Foulsham. *Norf* 3D **9**
Four Ashes. *Suff* 2D **25**
Four Gotes. *Cambs* 1B **14**
Fowlmere. *Cambs* 2B **30**
Foxearth. *Essx* 2B **32**
Fox Hatch. *Essx* 3C **39**
Foxley. *Norf* 3D **9**
Fox Street. *Essx* 1D **41**
Foxton. *Cambs* 2B **30**
Framingham Earl. *Norf* ...2B **18**
Framingham Pigot.
      Norf 2B **18**
Framlingham. *Suff* 3B **26**
Frampton. *Linc* 2A **6**
Frampton West End.
      Linc 1D **5**
Framsden. *Suff* 1A **34**
Frankfort. *Norf* 3C **11**
Frating Green. *Essx* 1D **41**
Freckenham. *Suff* 2D **23**
Freethorpe. *Norf* 2D **19**
Freiston. *Linc* 1A **6**
Freiston Shore. *Linc* 1A **6**
Frenze. *Norf* 1A **26**
Fressingfield. *Suff* 2B **26**
Freston. *Suff* 3A **34**
Frettenham. *Norf* 1B **18**
Friday Bridge. *Cambs* 2B **14**
Frieston. *Linc* 1A **4**
Fring. *Norf* 2A **8**
Frinton-on-Sea. *Essx* ...2B **42**
Friston. *Suff* 3D **27**
Frith Bank. *Linc* 1A **6**

Frithsden. *Herts* 3B **36**
Frithville. *Linc* 1A **6**
Fritton. *Norf* 2D **19**
      (nr. Great Yarmouth)
Fritton. *Norf* 3B **18**
      (nr. Long Stratton)
Frogmore. *Herts* 3C **37**
Frognall. *Linc* 1C **13**
Frogshall. *Norf* 2B **10**
Froxfield. *Beds* 3A **28**
Fryerning. *Essx* 3D **39**
Fulbeck. *Linc* 1A **4**
Fulbourn. *Cambs* 1C **31**
Fuller Street. *Essx* 2A **40**
Fulmodestone. *Norf* 2C **9**
Fulney. *Linc* 3D **5**
Fundenhall. *Norf* 3A **18**
Furneux Pelham. *Herts* ...1B **38**
Fyfield. *Essx* 3C **39**

G

Gainsborough. *Suff* 2A **34**
Gainsford End. *Essx* 3A **32**
Galleyend. *Essx* 3A **40**
Galleywood. *Essx* 3A **40**
Gamlingay. *Cambs* 1D **29**
Gamlingay Cinques.
      Cambs 1D **29**
Gamlingay Great Heath.
      Cambs 1D **29**
Garboldisham. *Norf* 1D **25**
Garnsgate. *Linc* 3B **6**
Garvestone. *Norf* 2D **17**
Garwick. *Linc* 1C **5**
Gasthorpe. *Norf* 1C **25**
Gateley. *Norf* 3C **9**
Gaultree. *Norf* 2B **14**
Gay Bowers. *Essx* 3A **40**
Gayhurst. *Mil* 2A **28**
Gayton. *Norf* 1A **16**
Gayton Thorpe. *Norf* 1A **16**
Gaywood. *Norf* 3D **7**
Gazeley. *Suff* 3A **24**
Gedding. *Suff* 1C **33**
Geddington. *Nptn* 1A **20**
Gedney. *Linc* 3B **6**
Gedney Broadgate. *Linc* ...3B **6**
Gedney Drove End. *Linc* ...3B **6**
Gedney Dyke. *Linc* 3B **6**
Gedney Hill. *Linc* 1A **14**
Geeston. *Rut* 2A **12**
Geldeston. *Norf* 3C **19**
Gelston. *Linc* 1A **4**
Gestingthorpe. *Essx* 3B **32**
Gibraltar. *Suff* 1A **34**
Gillingham. *Norf* 3D **19**
Gimingham. *Norf* 2B **10**
Gipping. *Suff* 3D **25**
Gipsey Bridge. *Linc* 1D **5**
Girton. *Cambs* 3B **22**
Gisleham. *Suff* 1D **27**
Gislingham. *Suff* 2D **25**
Gissing. *Norf* 1A **26**
Glandford. *Norf* 1D **9**
Glapthorn. *Nptn* 3B **12**
Glaston. *Rut* 2A **12**
Glatton. *Cambs* 1C **21**
Glemsford. *Suff* 2B **32**
Glinton. *Pet* 2C **13**
Goddard's Corner. *Suff* ...3B **26**
Godmanchester.
      Cambs 2D **21**
Goff's Oak. *Herts* 3A **38**
Goldhanger. *Essx* 3C **41**
Gold Hill. *Norf* 3C **15**
Goldington. *Beds* 1B **28**
Gonerby Hill Foot. *Linc* ...2A **4**
Good Easter. *Essx* 2D **39**
Gooderstone. *Norf* 2A **16**

Gorefield. *Cambs* 1B **14**
Gorleston-on-Sea. *Norf* ...2D **19**
Gosbeck. *Suff* 1A **34**
Gosberton. *Linc* 2D **5**
Gosberton Clough. *Linc* ...3C **5**
Gosfield. *Essx* 1A **40**
Gosmore. *Herts* 1C **37**
Graby. *Linc* 3B **4**
Grafham. *Cambs* 3C **21**
Grafton Underwood.
      Nptn 1A **20**
Grantchester. *Cambs* 1B **30**
Grantham. *Linc* 2A **4**
Graveley. *Cambs* 3D **21**
Graveley. *Herts* 1D **37**
Great Abington. *Cambs* ...2C **31**
Great Addington. *Nptn* ...2A **20**
Great Amwell. *Herts* 2A **38**
Great Ashfield. *Suff* 3C **25**
Great Baddow. *Essx* 3A **40**
Great Bardfield. *Essx* 3D **31**
Great Barford. *Beds* 1C **29**
Great Barton. *Suff* 3B **24**
Great Bealings. *Suff* 2B **34**
Great Bentley. *Essx* 1A **42**
Great Bircham. *Norf* 2A **8**
Great Blakenham. *Suff* ...1A **34**
Great Bradley. *Suff* 1D **31**
Great Braxted. *Essx* 2B **40**
Great Bricett. *Suff* 1D **33**
Great Brickhill. *Buck* 3A **28**
Great Bromley. *Essx* 1D **41**
Great Canfield. *Essx* 2C **39**
Great Casterton. *Rut* 2B **12**
Great Chesterford.
      Essx 2C **31**
Great Chishill. *Cambs* 3B **30**
Great Clacton. *Essx* 2A **42**
Great Cornard. *Suff* 2B **32**
Great Cressingham.
      Norf 2B **16**
Great Doddington.
      Nptn 3A **20**
Great Dunham. *Norf* 1B **16**
Great Dunmow. *Essx* 1D **39**
Great Easton. *Essx* 1D **39**
Great Easton. *Leics* 3A **12**
Great Ellingham. *Norf* ...3D **17**
Great Eversden. *Cambs* ...1A **30**
Great Finborough. *Suff* ...1D **33**
Greatford. *Linc* 1B **12**
Great Fransham. *Norf* ...1B **16**
Great Gaddesden.
      Herts 2B **36**
Great Gidding. *Cambs* ...1C **21**
Great Glemham. *Suff* 3C **27**
Great Gonerby. *Linc* 2A **4**
Great Gransden.
      Cambs 1D **29**
Great Green. *Norf* 1B **26**
Great Green. *Suff* 1C **33**
      (nr. Lavenham)
Great Green. *Suff* 1C **33**
      (nr. Palgrave)
Great Hale. *Linc* 1C **5**
Great Hallingbury. *Essx* ...2C **39**
Great Hampden. *Buck* ...3A **36**
Great Harrowden. *Nptn* ...2A **20**
Great Henny. *Essx* 3B **32**
Great Hockham. *Norf* ...3C **17**
Great Holland. *Essx* 2B **42**
Great Horkesley. *Essx* ...3C **33**
Great Hormead. *Herts* ...3B **30**
Great Kingshill. *Buck* 3A **36**
Great Leighs. *Essx* 2A **40**
Great Linford. *Mil* 2A **28**
Great Livermere. *Suff* ...2B **24**
Great Maplestead. *Essx* ...3B **32**
Great Massingham. *Norf* ..3A **8**
Great Melton. *Norf* 2A **18**
Great Missenden. *Buck* ...3A **36**

Great Moulton. *Norf* 3A **18**
Great Munden. *Herts* 1A **38**
Great Notley. *Essx* 1A **40**
Great Oakley. *Essx* 1A **42**
Great Oakley. *Nptn* 1A **20**
Great Offley. *Herts* 1C **37**
Great Oxney Green.
      Essx 3D **39**
Great Parndon. *Essx* 3B **38**
Great Paxton. *Cambs* 3D **21**
Great Plumstead. *Norf* ...1C **19**
Great Ponton. *Linc* 2A **4**
Great Raveley. *Cambs* 1D **21**
Great Ryburgh. *Norf* 3C **9**
Great Saling. *Essx* 1D **39**
Great Sampford. *Essx* 3D **31**
Great Saxham. *Suff* 3A **24**
Great Shelford. *Cambs* ...1B **30**
Great Snoring. *Norf* 2C **9**
Great Staughton.
      Cambs 3C **21**
Great Stukeley. *Cambs* ...2D **21**
Great Tey. *Essx* 1B **40**
Great Thurlow. *Suff* 1D **31**
Great Totham North.
      Essx 2B **40**
Great Totham South.
      Essx 2B **40**
Great Waldingfield.
      Suff 2C **33**
Great Walsingham. *Norf* ...2C **9**
Great Waltham. *Essx* 2D **39**
Great Wenham. *Suff* 3D **33**
Great Whelnetham.
      Suff 1B **32**
Great Wigborough. *Essx*. . .2C **41**
Great Wilbraham.
      Cambs 1C **31**
Great Witchingham.
      Norf 3A **10**
Great Wratting. *Suff* 2D **31**
Great Wymondley.
      Herts 1D **37**
Great Yarmouth.
      Norf ....2D **19 & 58**
Great Yeldham. *Essx* 3A **32**
Green End. *Beds* 2B **28**
Green End. *Herts* 3A **30**
      (nr. Buntingford)
Green End. *Herts* 1A **38**
      (nr. Stevenage)
Greenfield. *Beds* 3B **28**
Greengate. *Norf* 1D **17**
Greensgate. *Norf* 1A **18**
Greenstead Green.
      Essx 1B **40**
Greensted Green.
      Essx 3C **39**
Green Street. *Herts* 3C **37**
Green Street. *Suff* 2A **26**
Greenstreet Green.
      Suff 2D **33**
Green Tye. *Herts* 2B **38**
Greetham. *Rut* 1A **12**
Grendon. *Nptn* 3A **20**
Gresham. *Norf* 2A **10**
Gressenhall. *Norf* 1C **17**
Gretton. *Nptn* 3A **12**
Grimsthorpe. *Linc* 3B **4**
Grimston. *Norf* 3A **8**
Grimstone End. *Suff* 3C **25**
Griston. *Norf* 3C **17**
Gromford. *Suff* 1C **35**
Groton. *Suff* 2C **33**
Grundisburgh. *Suff* 1B **34**
Gubblecote. *Herts* 2A **36**
Guestwick. *Norf* 3D **9**
Guestwick Green. *Norf* ...3D **9**
Guilden Morden.
      Cambs 2D **29**
Guist. *Norf* 3C **9**

Gulling Green—How End

Gulling Green. *Suff* 1B **32**
Gunby. *Linc* 3A **4**
Gunthorpe. *Norf* 2D **9**
Gunthorpe. *Pet* 2C **13**
Guthram Gowt. *Linc* 3C **5**
Guyhirn. *Cambs* 2B **14**
Guyhirn Gull. *Cambs* 2A **14**
Guy's Head. *Linc* 3B **6**

H

Hacconby. *Linc* 3C **5**
Haceby. *Linc* 2B **4**
Hacheston. *Suff* 1C **35**
Hackford. *Norf* 2D **17**
Haddenham. *Cambs* 2B **22**
Haddenham End. *Cambs* 2B **22**
Haddiscoe. *Norf* 3D **19**
Haddon. *Cambs* 3C **13**
Hadham Cross. *Herts* 2B **38**
Hadham Ford. *Herts* 1B **38**
Hadleigh. *Suff* 2D **33**
Hadleigh Heath. *Suff* 2C **33**
Hadley Wood. *G Lon* 3D **37**
Hadstock. *Essx* 2C **31**
Hailey. *Herts* 2A **38**
Hail Weston. *Cambs* 3C **21**
Hainford. *Norf* 1B **18**
Hales. *Norf* 3C **19**
Halesgate. *Linc* 3A **6**
Halesworth. *Suff* 2C **27**
Hall End. *Beds* 2B **28**
Hall Green. *Norf* 1A **26**
Hall's Green. *Herts* 1D **37**
Halstead. *Essx* 3B **32**
Haltoft End. *Linc* 1A **6**
Halton. *Buck* 3A **36**
Halvergate. *Norf* 2D **19**
Hamerton. *Cambs* 2C **21**
Hammond Street. *Herts* 3A **38**
Hamperden End. *Essx* 3C **31**
Hampton Hargate. *Pet* 3C **13**
Hamrow. *Norf* 3C **9**
Hanby. *Linc* 2B **4**
Hanscombe End. *Beds* 3C **29**
Hanthorpe. *Linc* 3B **4**
Hanworth. *Norf* 2A **10**
Happisburgh. *Norf* 2C **11**
Happisburgh Common. *Norf* 3C **11**
Hapton. *Norf* 3A **18**
Hardingham. *Norf* 2D **17**
Hardley Street. *Norf* 2C **19**
Hardmead. *Mil* 2A **28**
Hardwick. *Cambs* 1A **30**
Hardwick. *Norf* 1B **26**
Hardwick. *Nptn* 3A **20**
Hardy's Green. *Essx* 1C **41**
Hare Green. *Essx* 1D **41**
Hare Street. *Essx* 3B **38**
Hare Street. *Herts* 1A **38**
Hargate. *Norf* 3A **18**
Hargrave. *Nptn* 2B **20**
Hargrave. *Suff* 1A **32**
Harkstead. *Suff* 3A **34**
Harlaxton. *Linc* 2A **4**
Harleston. *Norf* 1B **26**
Harleston. *Suff* 3D **25**
Harling Road. *Norf* 1C **25**
Harlington. *Beds* 3B **28**
Harlow. *Essx* 2B **38**
Harlton. *Cambs* 1A **30**
Harmer Green. *Herts* 2D **37**
Harpenden. *Herts* 2C **37**
Harpley. *Norf* 3A **8**
Harringworth. *Nptn* 3A **12**
Harrold. *Beds* 1A **28**
Harrowden. *Beds* 2B **28**
Harston. *Cambs* 1B **30**
Harston. *Leics* 2A **4**
Hartest. *Suff* 1B **32**
Hartford. *Cambs* 2D **21**
Hartford End. *Essx* 2D **39**
Harwich. *Essx* 3B **34**
Hasketon. *Suff* 1B **34**
Haslingfield. *Cambs* 1B **30**
Hassingham. *Norf* 2C **19**
Hastingwood. *Essx* 3B **38**
Hastoe. *Herts* 3A **36**
Hatch. *Beds* 2C **29**
Hatching Green. *Herts* 2C **37**
Hatfield. *Herts* 3D **37**
Hatfield Broad Oak. *Essx* 2C **39**
Hatfield Heath. *Essx* 2C **39**
Hatfield Hyde. *Herts* 2D **37**
Hatfield Peverel. *Essx* 2A **40**
Hatley St George. *Cambs* 1D **29**
Haughley. *Suff* 3D **25**
Haughley Green. *Suff* 3D **25**
Haultwick. *Herts* 1A **38**
Hauxton. *Cambs* 1B **30**
Haven Bank. *Linc* 1D **5**
Haverhill. *Suff* 2D **31**
Hawes Green. *Norf* 3B **18**
Hawkedon. *Suff* 1A **32**
Hawstead. *Suff* 1B **32**
Hawthorpe. *Linc* 3B **4**
Hay Green. *Norf* 1C **15**
Haynes. *Beds* 2B **28**
Haynes West End. *Beds* 2B **28**
Hay Street. *Herts* 1A **38**
Hazeleigh. *Essx* 3B **40**
Heacham. *Norf* 2D **7**
Heath and Reach. *Beds* 1A **36**
Heath, The. *Norf* 3B **10** (nr. Buxton)
Heath, The. *Norf* 3C **9** (nr. Fakenham)
Heath, The. *Norf* 3A **10** (nr. Heavingham)
Heathton. *Suff* 3A **34**
Hebing End. *Herts* 1A **38**
Heckfield Green. *Suff* 2A **26**
Heckfordbridge. *Essx* 1C **41**
Heckington. *Linc* 1C **5**
Hedenham. *Norf* 3C **19**
Helhoughton. *Norf* 3B **8**
Helions Bumpstead. *Essx* 2D **31**
Hellesdon. *Norf* 1B **18**
Hellington. *Norf* 2C **19**
Helmingham. *Suff* 1A **34**
Helpringham. *Linc* 1C **5**
Helpston. *Pet* 2C **13**
Hemblington. *Norf* 1C **19**
Hemel Hempstead. *Herts* 3B **36**
Hemingford Abbots. *Cambs* 2D **21**
Hemingford Grey. *Cambs* 2D **21**
Hemingstone. *Suff* 1A **34**
Hemington. *Nptn* 1B **20**
Hemley. *Suff* 2B **34**
Hempnall. *Norf* 3B **18**
Hempnall Green. *Norf* 3B **18**
Hemp's Green. *Essx* 1C **41**
Hempstead. *Essx* 3D **31**
Hempstead. *Norf* 2A **10** (nr. Holt)
Hempstead. *Norf* 3D **11** (nr. Stalham)
Hempton. *Norf* 3C **9**
Hemsby. *Norf* 1D **19**
Hengrave. *Suff* 3B **24**
Henham. *Essx* 1C **39**
Henley. *Suff* 1A **34**
Henlow. *Beds* 3C **29**
Henny Street. *Essx* 3B **32**
Henstead. *Suff* 1D **27**
Hepworth. *Suff* 2C **25**
Herringfleet. *Suff* 3D **19**
Herringswell. *Suff* 3A **24**
Hertford. *Herts* 2A **38**
Hertford Heath. *Herts* 2A **38**
Hertingfordbury. *Herts* 2A **38**
Hessett. *Suff* 3C **25**
Hethersett. *Norf* 2A **18**
Heveningham. *Suff* 2C **27**
Hevingham. *Norf* 3A **10**
Hexton. *Herts* 3C **29**
Heybridge. *Essx* 3D **39** (nr. Brentwood)
Heybridge. *Essx* 3B **40** (nr. Maldon)
Heybridge Basin. *Essx* 3B **40**
Heydon. *Cambs* 2B **30**
Heydon. *Norf* 3A **10**
Heydour. *Linc* 2B **4**
Hickling. *Norf* 3D **11**
Hickling Green. *Norf* 3D **11**
Hickling Heath. *Norf* 3D **11**
Higham. *Suff* 3D **33** (nr. Ipswich)
Higham. *Suff* 3A **24** (nr. Newmarket)
Higham Ferrers. *Nptn* 3A **20**
Higham Gobion. *Beds* 3C **29**
High Barnet. *G Lon* 3D **37**
High Beech. *Essx* 3B **38**
High Common. *Norf* 2C **17**
High Cross. *Herts* 2A **38**
High Easter. *Essx* 2D **39**
High Ferry. *Linc* 1A **6**
Highfields. *Cambs* 1A **30**
High Garrett. *Essx* 1A **40**
High Green. *Norf* 2A **18**
High Kelling. *Norf* 1A **10**
High Laver. *Essx* 3C **39**
High Ongar. *Essx* 3C **39**
High Roding. *Essx* 2D **39**
High Street. *Suff* 1D **35** (nr. Aldeburgh)
High Street. *Suff* 1C **27** (nr. Bungay)
High Street. *Suff* 2D **27** (nr. Yoxford)
Highstreet Green. *Essx* 3A **32**
High Street Green. *Suff* 1D **33**
Hightown Green. *Suff* 1C **33**
High Wych. *Herts* 2B **38**
Hilborough. *Norf* 2B **16**
Hildersham. *Cambs* 2C **31**
Hilgay. *Norf* 3D **15**
Hilldyke. *Linc* 1A **6**
Hill Green. *Essx* 3B **30**
Hillington. *Norf* 3A **8**
Hilton. *Cambs* 3D **21**
Hinderclay. *Suff* 2D **25**
Hindolveston. *Norf* 3D **9**
Hindringham. *Norf* 2C **9**
Hingham. *Norf* 2D **17**
Hintlesham. *Suff* 2D **33**
Hinwick. *Beds* 3A **20**
Hinxton. *Cambs* 2B **30**
Hinxworth. *Herts* 2D **29**
Histon. *Cambs* 3B **22**
Hitcham. *Suff* 1C **33**
Hitchin. *Herts* 1C **37**
Hobbles Green. *Suff* 1A **32**
Hobbs Cross. *Essx* 3B **38**
Hockering. *Norf* 1D **17**
Hockering Heath. *Norf* 1D **17**
Hockliffe. *Beds* 1A **36**
Hockwold cum Wilton. *Norf* 1A **24**
Hoddesdon. *Herts* 3A **38**
Hoe. *Norf* 1C **17**
Hoffleet Stow. *Linc* 2D **5**
Hoggard's Green. *Suff* 1B **32**
Holbeach. *Linc* 3A **6**
Holbeach Bank. *Linc* 3A **6**
Holbeach Clough. *Linc* 3A **6**
Holbeach Drove. *Linc* 1A **14**
Holbeach Hurn. *Linc* 3A **6**
Holbeach St Johns. *Linc* 1A **14**
Holbeach St Marks. *Linc* 2A **6**
Holbeach St Matthew. *Linc* 2B **6**
Holbrook. *Suff* 3A **34**
Holder's Green. *Essx* 1D **39**
Holdingham. *Linc* 1B **4**
Holkham. *Norf* 1B **8**
Holland Fen. *Linc* 1D **5**
Holland-on-Sea. *Essx* 2B **42**
Hollesley. *Suff* 2C **35**
Hollingdon. *Buck* 1A **36**
Holly End. *Norf* 2B **14**
Holme. *Cambs* 1C **21**
Holme Hale. *Norf* 2B **16**
Holme next the Sea. *Norf* 1A **8**
Holmer Green. *Buck* 3A **36**
Holmsey Green. *Suff* 2D **23**
Holt. *Norf* 2D **9**
Holton. *Suff* 2C **27**
Holton St Mary. *Suff* 3D **33**
Holtsmere End. *Herts* 2B **36**
Holwell. *Herts* 3C **29**
Holyfield. *Essx* 3A **38**
Holywell. *Cambs* 2A **22**
Holywell Row. *Suff* 2A **24**
Homersfield. *Suff* 1B **26**
Honey Tye. *Suff* 3C **33**
Honeywick. *Beds* 1A **36**
Honing. *Norf* 3C **11**
Honingham. *Norf* 1A **18**
Honington. *Linc* 1A **4**
Honington. *Suff* 2C **25**
Hoo. *Suff* 1B **34**
Hook. *Cambs* 3B **14**
Hook's Cross. *Herts* 1D **37**
Hop Pole. *Linc* 1C **13**
Hopton. *Suff* 2C **25**
Hopton on Sea. *Norf* 2D **19**
Horbling. *Linc* 2C **5**
Horham. *Suff* 2B **26**
Horkesley Heath. *Essx* 1C **41**
Horning. *Norf* 1C **19**
Horningsea. *Cambs* 3B **22**
Horningtoft. *Norf* 3C **9**
Horringer. *Suff* 3B **24**
Horseheath. *Cambs* 2D **31**
Horseway. *Cambs* 1B **22**
Horsey. *Norf* 3D **11**
Horsford. *Norf* 1A **18**
Horsham St Faith. *Norf* 1B **18**
Horsley Cross. *Essx* 1A **42**
Horsleycross Street. *Essx* 1A **42**
Horstead. *Norf* 1B **18**
Horton. *Buck* 2A **36**
Hougham. *Linc* 1A **4**
Hough-on-the-Hill. *Linc* 1A **4**
Houghton. *Cambs* 2D **21**
Houghton Conquest. *Beds* 2B **28**
Houghton Regis. *Beds* 1B **36**
Houghton St Giles. *Norf* 2C **9**
Hoveton. *Norf* 1C **19**
Howe. *Norf* 2B **18**
Howe Green. *Essx* 3A **40** (nr. Chelmsford)
Howegreen. *Essx* 3B **40** (nr. Maldon)
Howell. *Linc* 1C **5**
How End. *Beds* 2B **28**

Howe Street. Essx ... 2D 39
(nr. Chelmsford)
Howe Street. Essx ... 3D 31
(nr. Finchingfield)
How Hill. Norf ... 1C 19
Howlett End. Essx ... 3C 31
Hoxne. Suff ... 2A 26
Hubbert's Bridge. Linc ... 1D 5
Hughenden Valley.
Buck ... 3A 36
Hulcott. Buck ... 2A 36
Hulver Street. Suff ... 1D 27
Humby. Linc ... 2B 4
Hundle Houses. Linc ... 1D 5
Hundon. Suff ... 2A 32
Hungerton. Linc ... 2A 4
Hunsdon. Herts ... 2B 38
Hunstanton. Norf ... 1D 7
Hunston. Suff ... 3C 25
Huntingdon. Cambs ... 2D 21
Huntingfield. Suff ... 2D 25
Hunton Bridge. Herts ... 3B 36
Hunt's Corner. Norf ... 1D 25
Hunworth. Norf ... 2D 9
Hurst Green. Essx ... 2D 41
Husborne Crawley.
Beds ... 3A 28
Hyde Heath. Buck ... 3A 36

I

Ickburgh. Norf ... 3B 16
Ickleford. Herts ... 3C 29
Ickleton. Cambs ... 2B 30
Icklingham. Suff ... 2A 24
Ickwell. Beds ... 2C 29
Iken. Suff ... 1D 35
Ilketshall St Andrew.
Suff ... 1C 27
Ilketshall St Lawrence.
Suff ... 1C 27
Ilketshall St Margaret.
Suff ... 1C 27
Illington. Norf ... 1C 25
Impington. Cambs ... 3B 22
Ingatestone. Essx ... 3D 39
Ingham. Norf ... 3C 11
Ingham. Suff ... 2B 24
Ingham Corner. Norf ... 3C 11
Ingleborough. Norf ... 1B 14
Ingoldisthorpe. Norf ... 2D 7
Ingoldsby. Linc ... 2B 4
Ingthorpe. Rut ... 2A 12
Ingworth. Norf ... 3A 10
Intwood. Norf ... 2A 18
Ipworth. Essx ... 2B 40
Ipswich. Suff ... 2A 34 & 58
Irchester. Nptn ... 3A 20
Irnham. Linc ... 3B 4
Iron Bridge. Cambs ... 3B 14
Irstead. Norf ... 3C 11
Irthlingborough. Nptn ... 2A 20
Isham. Nptn ... 2A 20
Isleham. Cambs ... 2D 23
Islip. Nptn ... 2A 20
Iteringham. Norf ... 2A 10
Iteringham Common.
Norf ... 3A 10
Ivinghoe. Buck ... 2A 36
Ivinghoe Aston. Buck ... 2A 36
Ivy Todd. Norf ... 2B 16
Ixworth. Suff ... 2C 25
Ixworth Thorpe. Suff ... 2C 25

J

Jasper's Green. Essx ... 1A 40
Jaywick. Essx ... 2A 42
Jockey End. Herts ... 2B 36

Johnson's Street. Norf ... 1C 19
Jordan Green. Norf ... 3D 9

K

Kedington. Suff ... 2A 32
Keeley Green. Beds ... 2B 28
Keisby. Linc ... 3B 4
Kelby. Linc ... 1B 4
Kelling. Norf ... 1D 9
Kelsale. Suff ... 3C 27
Kelshall. Herts ... 3A 30
Kelvedon. Essx ... 2B 40
Kelvedon Hatch. Essx ... 3C 39
Kempston. Beds ... 2B 28
Kempston Hardwick.
Beds ... 2B 28
Kennett. Cambs ... 3A 24
Kenninghall. Norf ... 1D 25
Kennyhill. Suff ... 2D 23
Kensworth. Beds ... 2B 36
Kensworth Common.
Beds ... 2B 36
Kentford. Suff ... 3A 24
Kenton. Suff ... 3A 26
Kersey. Suff ... 2D 33
Kesgrave. Suff ... 2B 34
Kessingland. Suff ... 1D 27
Kessingland Beach.
Suff ... 1D 27
Keswick. Norf ... 2C 11
(nr. North Walsham)
Keswick. Norf ... 2B 18
(nr. Norwich)
Kettering. Nptn ... 2A 20
Ketteringham. Norf ... 2A 18
Kettlebaston. Suff ... 1C 33
Kettleburgh. Suff ... 3B 26
Kettlestone. Norf ... 2C 9
Ketton. Rut ... 2A 12
Keysoe. Beds ... 3B 20
Keysoe Row. Beds ... 3B 20
Keyston. Cambs ... 2B 20
Kidd's Moor. Norf ... 2A 18
Kimberley. Norf ... 2D 17
Kimbolton. Cambs ... 3B 20
Kimpton. Herts ... 2C 37
Kingsash. Buck ... 3A 36
King's Cliffe. Nptn ... 3B 12
Kingshall Street. Suff ... 3C 25
Kings Langley. Herts ... 3B 36
King's Lynn. Norf ... 3D 7 & 58
Kings Ripton. Cambs ... 2D 21
Kingston. Cambs ... 1A 30
King's Walden. Herts ... 1C 37
Kinsbourne Green.
Herts ... 2C 37
Kirby Bedon. Norf ... 2B 18
Kirby Cane. Norf ... 3C 19
Kirby Cross. Essx ... 1B 42
Kirby-le-Soken. Essx ... 1B 42
Kirby Row. Norf ... 3C 19
Kirkby la Thorpe. Linc ... 1C 5
Kirkby Underwood.
Linc ... 3B 4
Kirkley. Suff ... 3D 19
Kirstead Green. Norf ... 3B 18
Kirtling. Cambs ... 1D 31
Kirtling Green. Cambs ... 1D 31
Kirton. Linc ... 2A 6
Kirton. Suff ... 3B 34
Kirton End. Linc ... 1D 5
Kirton Holme. Linc ... 1D 5
Knapton. Norf ... 2C 11
Knapwell. Cambs ... 3A 22
Knebworth. Herts ... 1D 37
Kneesworth. Cambs ... 2A 30
Knight's End. Cambs ... 3B 14
Knodishall. Suff ... 3D 27
Knotting. Beds ... 3B 20

Knotting Green. Beds ... 3B 20
Knuston. Nptn ... 3A 20

L

Lackford. Suff ... 2A 24
Lakenham. Norf ... 2B 18
Lakenheath. Suff ... 1A 24
Lakesend. Norf ... 3C 15
Lamarsh. Essx ... 3B 32
Lamas. Norf ... 3B 10
Lamb Corner. Essx ... 3D 33
Landbeach. Cambs ... 3B 22
Langenhoe. Essx ... 2D 41
Langford. Beds ... 2C 29
Langford. Essx ... 3B 40
Langham. Essx ... 3D 33
Langham. Norf ... 1D 9
Langham. Rut ... 1A 12
Langham. Suff ... 3C 25
Langley. Essx ... 3B 30
Langley. Herts ... 1D 37
Langleybury. Herts ... 3B 36
Langley Green. Norf ... 2C 19
Langley Street. Norf ... 2C 19
Langrick. Linc ... 1D 5
Langtoft. Linc ... 1C 13
Larling. Norf ... 1C 25
Latchford. Herts ... 1A 38
Latchingdon. Essx ... 3B 40
Lathbury. Mil ... 2A 28
Latimer. Buck ... 3B 36
Laughton. Linc ... 2B 4
Lavendon. Mil ... 1A 28
Lavenham. Suff ... 2C 33
Lawford. Essx ... 3D 33
Lawshall. Suff ... 1B 32
Laxfield. Suff ... 2B 26
Laxton. Nptn ... 3A 12
Layer Breton. Essx ... 2C 41
Layer-de-la-Haye. Essx ... 1C 41
Layer Marney. Essx ... 2C 41
Leadenham. Linc ... 1A 4
Leaden Roding. Essx ... 2C 39
Leagrave. Lutn ... 1B 36
Leake Common Side.
Linc ... 1A 6
Leake Fold Hill. Linc ... 1B 6
Leake Hurn's End. Linc ... 1B 6
Leasingham. Linc ... 1B 4
Leavenheath. Suff ... 3C 33
Ledburn. Buck ... 1A 36
Lee Clump. Buck ... 3A 36
Lee, The. Buck ... 3A 36
Leighton Bromswold.
Cambs ... 2C 21
Leighton Buzzard.
Beds ... 1A 36
Leiston. Suff ... 3D 27
Lemsford. Herts ... 2D 37
Lenton. Linc ... 2B 4
Lenwade. Norf ... 1D 17
Lessingham. Norf ... 3C 11
Letchmore Heath.
Herts ... 3C 37
Letchworth Garden City.
Herts ... 3D 29
Letheringham. Suff ... 1B 34
Letheringsett. Norf ... 2D 9
Letty Green. Herts ... 2D 37
Levens Green. Herts ... 1A 38
Leverington. Cambs ... 1B 14
Leverton. Linc ... 1A 6
Leverton Lucasgate.
Linc ... 1B 6
Leverton Outgate. Linc ... 1B 6
Levington. Suff ... 3B 34
Ley Green. Herts ... 1C 37
Ley Hill. Buck ... 3A 36
Leziate. Norf ... 1D 15

Lidgate. Suff ... 1A 32
Lidlington. Beds ... 3A 28
Lilley. Herts ... 1C 37
Limbury. Lutn ... 1B 36
Limpenhoe. Norf ... 2C 19
Lindsell. Essx ... 1D 39
Lindsey. Suff ... 2C 33
Lindsey Tye. Suff ... 2C 33
Ling, The. Norf ... 3C 19
Lingwood. Norf ... 2C 19
Linslade. Beds ... 1A 36
Linstead Parva. Suff ... 2C 27
Linton. Cambs ... 2C 31
Liston. Essx ... 2B 32
Litcham. Norf ... 1B 16
Litlington. Cambs ... 2A 30
Little Abington. Cambs ... 2C 31
Little Addington. Nptn ... 2A 20
Little Baddow. Essx ... 3A 40
Little Bardfield. Essx ... 3D 31
Little Barford. Beds ... 1C 29
Little Barningham.
Norf ... 2A 10
Little Bealings. Suff ... 2B 34
Little Bentley. Essx ... 1A 42
Little Berkhamsted.
Herts ... 3D 37
Little Billington. Beds ... 1A 36
Little Blakenham. Suff ... 2A 34
Little Bradley. Suff ... 1D 31
Little Brickhill. Mil ... 3A 28
Little Bromley. Essx ... 1D 41
Littlebury. Essx ... 3C 31
Littlebury Green. Essx ... 3B 30
Little Bytham. Linc ... 1B 12
Little Canfield. Essx ... 1C 39
Little Casterton. Rut ... 2B 12
Little Catworth. Cambs ... 2C 21
Little Chalfont. Buck ... 3A 36
Little Chesterford. Essx ... 2C 31
Little Chishill. Cambs ... 3B 30
Little Clacton. Essx ... 2A 42
Little Cornard. Suff ... 3B 32
Little Crawley. Mil ... 2A 28
Little Cressingham.
Norf ... 2B 16
Little Ditton. Cambs ... 1D 31
Little Downham.
Cambs ... 1C 23
Little Dunham. Norf ... 1B 16
Little Dunmow. Essx ... 1D 39
Little Easton. Essx ... 1D 39
Little Ellingham. Norf ... 3D 17
Little End. Essx ... 3C 39
Little Eversden. Cambs ... 1A 30
Little Fransham. Norf ... 1C 17
Litle Gaddesden. Herts ... 2A 36
Little Gidding. Cambs ... 1C 21
Little Glemham. Suff ... 1C 35
Little Gransden. Cambs ... 1D 29
Little Hadham. Herts ... 1B 38
Little Hale. Linc ... 1C 5
Little Hallingbury. Essx ... 2B 38
Little Hampden. Buck ... 3A 36
Little Harrowden. Nptn ... 2A 20
Little Hautbois. Norf ... 3B 10
Little Horkesley. Essx ... 3C 33
Little Hormead. Herts ... 1B 38
Little Irchester. Nptn ... 3A 20
Little Kingshill. Buck ... 3A 36
Little Laver. Essx ... 3C 39
Little Leighs. Essx ... 2A 40
Little Linford. Mil ... 2A 28
Little London. Linc ... 3B 5
(nr. Long Sutton)
Little London. Linc ... 3D 5
(nr. Spalding)
Little London. Norf ... 2B 10
(nr. North Walsham)
Little London. Norf ... 3A 16
(nr. Northwold)

Little London. *Norf* 2A **10**
(nr. Saxthorpe)
Little London. *Norf* 3D **15**
(nr. Southery)
Little Maplestead. *Essx* . . . 3B **32**
Little Massingham. *Norf* . . . 3A **8**
Little Melton. *Norf* 2A **18**
Little Missenden. *Buck* . . . 3A **36**
Little Oakley. *Essx* 1B **42**
Little Oakley. *Nptn* 1A **20**
Little Ouse. *Norf* 1D **23**
Little Paxton. *Cambs* 3C **21**
Little Plumstead. *Norf* . . . 1C **19**
Little Ponton. *Linc* 2A **4**
Littleport. *Cambs* 1C **23**
Little Raveley. *Cambs* 2D **21**
Little Ryburgh. *Norf* 3C **9**
Little Sampford. *Essx* 3D **31**
Little Saxham. *Suff* 3A **24**
Little Shelford. *Cambs* . . . 1B **30**
Little Snoring. *Norf* 2C **9**
Little Staughton. *Beds* . . . 3C **21**
Little Stonham. *Suff* 3A **26**
Little Street. *Cambs* 1C **23**
Little Stukeley. *Cambs* . . . 2D **21**
Little Sutton. *Linc* 3B **6**
Little Tey. *Essx* 1B **40**
Little Thetford. *Cambs* . . . 2C **23**
Little Thurlow. *Suff* 1D **31**
Little Totham. *Essx* 2B **40**
Little Walden. *Essx* 2C **31**
Little Waldingfield. *Suff* . . 2C **33**
Little Walsingham. *Norf* . . 2C **9**
Little Waltham. *Essx* 2A **40**
Little Wenham. *Suff* 3D **33**
Little Whelnetham. *Suff* . . 1B **32**
Little Whittingham Green.
Suff 2B **26**
Little Wilbraham.
Cambs 1C **31**
Little Wisbeach. *Linc* 2C **5**
Littleworth. *Beds* 2B **28**
Little Wratting. *Suff* 2D **31**
Little Wymington. *Nptn* . . . 3A **20**
Little Wymondley.
Herts 1D **37**
Little Yeldham. *Essx* 3A **32**
Littley Green. *Essx* 2D **39**
Loddon. *Norf* 3C **19**
Lode. *Cambs* 3C **23**
Lolworth. *Cambs* 3A **22**
London Colney. *Herts* . . . 3C **37**
London Luton Airport.
Lutn 1C **37**
London Stansted Airport.
Essx 1C **39**
Londonthorpe. *Linc* 2A **4**
Long Gardens. *Essx* 3B **32**
Longham. *Norf* 1C **17**
Long Marston. *Herts* 2A **36**
Long Meadow. *Cambs* . . . 3C **23**
Long Melford. *Suff* 2B **32**
Longstanton. *Cambs* 3A **22**
Longstowe. *Cambs* 1A **30**
Long Stratton. *Norf* 3A **18**
Long Sutton. *Linc* 3B **6**
Longthorpe. *Pet* 3C **13**
Long Thurlow. *Suff* 3D **25**
Loosegate. *Linc* 3A **6**
Lound. *Linc* 1B **12**
Lound. *Suff* 3D **19**
Loves Green. *Essx* 3D **39**
Lower Benefield. *Nptn* . . . 1A **20**
Lower Dean. *Beds* 3B **20**
Lower East Carleton.
Norf 2A **18**
Lower End. *Nptn* 3A **20**
Lower Gravenhurst.
Beds 3C **29**
Lower Green. *Essx* 3B **30**
Lower Green. *Norf* 2C **9**

Lower Holbrook. *Suff* 3A **34**
Lower Layham. *Suff* 2D **33**
Lower Nazeing. *Essx* 3A **38**
Lower Raydon. *Suff* 3D **33**
Lower Shelton. *Beds* 2A **28**
Lower Stow Bedon.
Norf 3C **17**
Lower Street. *Norf* 2B **10**
Lower Sundon. *Beds* 1B **36**
Lower Thurlton. *Norf* 3D **19**
Lowestoft. *Suff* 3D **19**
Low Fulney. *Linc* 3D **5**
Lowick. *Nptn* 1A **20**
Low Street. *Norf* 2D **17**
Luddington in the Brook.
Nptn 1C **21**
Ludham. *Norf* 1C **19**
Luffenhall. *Herts* 1D **37**
Lundy Green. *Norf* 3B **18**
Luton. *Lutn* . . . . . . 1B **36** & **59**
Luton (London) Airport.
Lutn 1C **37**
Lutton. *Linc* 3B **6**
Lutton. *Nptn* 1C **21**
Lutton Gowts. *Linc* 3B **6**
Lyddington. *Rut* 3A **12**
Lye Green. *Buck* 3A **36**
Lynch Green. *Norf* 2A **18**
Lyndon. *Rut* 2A **12**
Lyng. *Norf* 1D **17**
Lyngate. *Norf* 2B **10**
(nr. North Walsham)
Lyngate. *Norf* 3C **11**
(nr. Worstead)

M

Mackerye End. *Herts* 2C **37**
Madingley. *Cambs* 3A **22**
Magdalen Laver. *Essx* . . . 3C **39**
Magpie Green. *Suff* 2D **25**
Maldon. *Essx* 3B **40**
Mallows Green. *Essx* 1B **38**
Manea. *Cambs* 1B **22**
Manningtree. *Essx* 3A **34**
Manthorpe. *Linc* 1B **12**
(nr. Bourne)
Manthorpe. *Linc* 2A **4**
(nr. Grantham)
Manton. *Rut* 2A **12**
Manuden. *Essx* 1B **38**
March. *Cambs* 3B **14**
Margaret Roding. *Essx* . . . 2C **39**
Margaretting. *Essx* 3D **39**
Margaretting Tye. *Essx* . . . 3D **39**
Marham. *Norf* 2A **16**
Marholm. *Pet* 2C **13**
Market Deeping. *Linc* . . . 1C **13**
Market Overton. *Rut* 1A **12**
Market Weston. *Suff* 2C **25**
Marks Tey. *Essx* 1C **41**
Markyate. *Herts* 2B **36**
Marlesford. *Suff* 1C **35**
Marlingford. *Norf* 2A **18**
Marshalswick. *Herts* 3C **37**
Marsham. *Norf* 3A **10**
Marsh Side. *Norf* 1A **8**
Marston. *Linc* 1A **4**
Marston Moretaine.
Beds 2A **28**
Marsworth. *Buck* 2A **36**
Martham. *Norf* 1D **19**
Martlesham. *Suff* 2B **34**
Martlesham Heath.
Suff 2B **34**
Mashbury. *Essx* 2D **39**
Matching. *Essx* 2C **39**
Matching Green. *Essx* . . . 2C **39**
Matching Tye. *Essx* 2C **39**
Matlaske. *Norf* 2A **10**

Mattishall. *Norf* 1D **17**
Mattishall Burgh. *Norf* . . . 1D **17**
Maulden. *Beds* 3B **28**
Mautby. *Norf* 1D **19**
Maxey. *Pet* 2C **13**
Mayland. *Essx* 3C **41**
Maylandsea. *Essx* 3C **41**
Maypole Green. *Norf* 3D **19**
Maypole Green. *Suff* 1C **33**
Meesden. *Herts* 3B **30**
Meeting Green. *Suff* 1A **32**
Melbourn. *Cambs* 2A **30**
Melchbourne. *Beds* 3B **20**
Meldreth. *Cambs* 2A **30**
Mellis. *Suff* 2D **25**
Melton. *Suff* 1B **34**
Melton Constable. *Norf* . . 2D **9**
Mendham. *Suff* 1B **26**
Mendlesham. *Suff* 3A **26**
Mendlesham Green.
Suff 3D **25**
Mentmore. *Buck* 2A **36**
Mepal. *Cambs* 1B **22**
Meppershall. *Beds* 3C **29**
Merton. *Norf* 3C **17**
Messing. *Essx* 2B **40**
Metfield. *Suff* 1B **26**
Methwold. *Norf* 3A **16**
Methwold Hythe. *Norf* . . . 3A **16**
Mettingham. *Suff* 3C **19**
Metton. *Norf* 2A **10**
Mickfield. *Suff* 3A **26**
Micklefield Green.
Herts 3B **36**
Mickley Green. *Suff* 1B **32**
Middle Harling. *Norf* 1C **25**
Middleton. *Essx* 3B **32**
Middleton. *Norf* 1D **15**
Middleton. *Suff* 3D **27**
Middlewood Green.
Suff 3D **25**
Milden. *Suff* 2C **33**
Mildenhall. *Suff* 2A **24**
Mile End. *Cambs* 1D **23**
Mile End. *Essx* 1C **41**
Mileham. *Norf* 1C **17**
Millbrook. *Beds* 3B **28**
Mill Common. *Suff* 1D **27**
Mill End. *Cambs* 1D **31**
Mill End. *Herts* 3A **30**
Millfield. *Pet* 3C **13**
Mill Green. *Essx* 3D **39**
Mill Green. *Norf* 1A **26**
Mill Green. *Suff* 2C **33**
Millow. *Beds* 2D **29**
Mill Street. *Norf* 1D **17**
(nr. Lyng)
Mill Street. *Norf* 1D **17**
(nr. Swanton Morley)
Mill Street. *Suff* 2D **25**
Millthorpe. *Linc* 2C **5**
Milton. *Cambs* 3B **22**
Milton Bryan. *Beds* 3A **28**
Milton Ernest. *Beds* 1B **28**
Milton Keynes. *Mil* . . . 3A **28**
Milton Keynes Village.
Mil 3A **28**
Mistley. *Essx* 3A **34**
Mistley Heath. *Essx* 3A **34**
Moats Tye. *Suff* 1D **33**
Moggerhanger. *Beds* 2C **29**
Molehill Green. *Essx* 1C **39**
Molesworth. *Cambs* 2B **20**
Monewden. *Suff* 1B **34**
Monken Hadley. *G Lon* . . 3D **37**
Monks Eleigh. *Suff* 2C **33**
Monk Soham. *Suff* 3B **26**
Monk Soham Green.
Suff 3B **26**
Monk Street. *Essx* 1D **39**
Morborne. *Cambs* 3C **13**

Morcott. *Rut* 2A **12**
Morely St Botolph.
Norf 3D **17**
Moreton. *Essx* 3C **39**
Morningthorpe. *Norf* 3B **18**
Morris Green. *Essx* 3A **32**
Morston. *Norf* 1D **9**
Morton. *Linc* 3B **4**
Morton. *Norf* 1A **18**
Moulsoe. *Mil* 2A **28**
Moulton. *Linc* 3A **6**
Moulton. *Suff* 3D **23**
Moulton Chapel. *Linc* . . . 1D **13**
Moulton Eugate. *Linc* . . . 1D **13**
Moulton St Mary. *Norf* . . . 2C **19**
Moulton Seas End. *Linc* . . 3A **6**
Mount Bures. *Essx* 3C **33**
Mountnessing. *Essx* 3D **39**
Mount Pleasant. *Norf* . . . 3C **17**
Much Hadham. *Herts* 2B **38**
Muckleton. *Norf* 2B **8**
Mulbarton. *Norf* 2A **18**
Mundesley. *Norf* 2C **11**
Mundford. *Norf* 3B **16**
Mundham. *Norf* 3C **19**
Mundon. *Essx* 3B **41**
Murrow. *Cambs* 2A **14**
Mutford. *Suff* 1D **27**

N

Nacton. *Suff* 2B **34**
Naphill. *Buck* 3A **36**
Narborough. *Norf* 1A **16**
Nash Lee. *Buck* 3A **36**
Nassington. *Nptn* 3B **12**
Nasty. *Herts* 1A **38**
Naughton. *Suff* 2D **33**
Navestock Heath. *Essx* . . 3C **39**
Navestock Side. *Essx* . . . 3C **39**
Nayland. *Suff* 3C **33**
Nazeing. *Essx* 3B **38**
Neatishead. *Norf* 3C **11**
Neaton. *Norf* 2C **17**
Necton. *Norf* 2B **16**
Nedging. *Suff* 2D **33**
Nedging Tye. *Suff* 2D **33**
Needham. *Norf* 1B **26**
Needham Market. *Suff* . . . 1D **33**
Needham Street. *Suff* . . . 3A **24**
Needingworth. *Cambs* . . . 2A **22**
Nene Terrace. *Linc* 2D **13**
Nethergate. *Norf* 3D **9**
Nether Street. *Essx* 2C **39**
Nettleden. *Herts* 2B **36**
Newark. *Pet* 2D **13**
Newborough. *Pet* 2D **13**
Newbourne. *Suff* 2B **34**
New Buckenham. *Norf* . . . 3D **17**
New Costessey. *Norf* 1A **18**
New England. *Essx* 2A **32**
New England. *Pet* 2C **13**
Newgate. *Norf* 1D **9**
Newgate Street. *Herts* . . . 3A **38**
New Greens. *Herts* 3C **37**
New Hainford. *Norf* 1B **18**
New Holkham. *Norf* 2B **8**
New Houghton. *Norf* 3A **8**
Newman's Green. *Suff* . . . 2B **32**
Newmarket. *Suff* 3D **23**
New Mill. *Herts* 2A **36**
New Mistley. *Essx* 3A **34**
Newnham. *Cambs* 1B **30**
Newnham. *Herts* 3D **29**
Newport. *Essx* 3C **31**
Newport. *Norf* 1D **19**
Newport Pagnell. *Mil* . . 2A **28**
New Rackheath. *Norf* 1B **18**
Newton. *Cambs* 2B **30**
(nr. Cambridge)

Newton. *Cambs* 1B **14**
(nr. Wisbech)
Newton. *Linc* 2B **4**
Newton. *Norf* 1B **16**
Newton. *Nptn* 1A **20**
Newton. *Suff* 2C **33**
Newton Blossomville.
Mil 1A **28**
Newton Bromswold.
Nptn 3A **20**
Newton Flotman. *Norf* . . 3B **18**
Newton Longville.
Buck 3A **28**
Newton St Faith. *Norf* . . . 1B **18**
Newtown. *Cambs* 3B **20**
New Town. *Lutn* 1B **36**
New Walsoken.
Cambs 2B **14**
New Wimpole. *Cambs* . . . 2A **30**
New World. *Cambs* 3A **14**
Nine Ashes. *Essx* 3C **39**
Nogdam End. *Norf* 2C **19**
Nordelph. *Norf* 2C **15**
Norman Cross.
Cambs 3C **13**
Normanton. *Linc* 1A **4**
North Acre. *Norf* 3C **17**
Northall. *Buck* 1A **36**
Northaw. *Herts* 3D **37**
North Barsham. *Norf* 2C **9**
Northbeck. *Linc* 1B **4**
Northborough. *Pet* 2C **13**
North Brook End.
Cambs 2D **29**
North Burlingham.
Norf 1C **19**
Northchurch. *Herts* 3A **36**
North Cove. *Suff* 1D **27**
North Crawley. *Mil* 2A **28**
North Creake. *Norf* 2B **8**
North Elmham. *Norf* 3C **9**
North End. *Essx* 2D **39**
(nr. Great Dunmow)
North End. *Essx* 3A **32**
(nr. Great Yeldham)
North End. *Linc* 1D **5**
North End. *Norf* 3C **17**
North Fambridge. *Essx* . . 3B **40**
Northgate. *Linc* 3C **5**
North Green. *Norf* 1B **26**
North Green. *Suff* 3C **27**
(nr. Framlingham)
North Green. *Suff* 2C **27**
(nr. Halesworth)
North Green. *Suff* 3C **27**
(nr. Saxmundham)
Northill. *Beds* 2C **29**
North Kyme. *Linc* 1C **5**
Northlands. *Linc* 1A **6**
North Lopham. *Norf* 1D **25**
North Luffenham. *Rut* . . . 2A **12**
Northorpe. *Linc* 1B **12**
(nr. Bourne)
Northorpe. *Linc* 2D **5**
(nr. Donington)
North Pickenham. *Norf* . . 2B **16**
North Rauceby. *Linc* 1B **4**
Northrepps. *Norf* 2B **10**
North Runcton. *Norf* 1D **15**
Northstowe. *Cambs* 3B **22**
North Tuddenham.
Norf 1D **17**
North Walsham. *Norf* . . . 2B **10**
North Weald Bassett.
Essx 3C **39**
North Witham. *Linc* 3A **4**
Northwold. *Norf* 3A **16**
North Wootton. *Norf* 3D **7**
Norton. *Herts* 3D **29**
Norton. *Suff* 3C **25**
Norton Corner. *Norf* 3D **9**

Norton Heath. *Essx* 3D **39**
Norton Little Green.
Suff 3C **25**
Norton Mandeville.
Essx 3C **39**
Norton Subcourse.
Norf 3D **19**
Norwich. *Norf* . . 2B **18** & **59**
Norwich International Airport.
Norf 1B **18**
Norwoodside. *Cambs* . . . 3B **14**
Nounsley. *Essx* 2A **40**
Nuthampstead. *Herts* . . . 3B **30**

O

Oakham. *Rut* 2A **12**
Oakington. *Cambs* 3B **22**
Oakley. *Beds* 1B **28**
Oakley. *Suff* 2A **26**
Oasby. *Linc* 2B **4**
Obthorpe. *Linc* 1B **12**
Occold. *Suff* 2A **26**
Odell. *Beds* 1A **28**
Odsey. *Cambs* 3D **29**
Offley Hoo. *Herts* 1C **37**
Offord Cluny. *Cambs* 3D **21**
Offord D'Arcy. *Cambs* . . . 3D **21**
Offton. *Suff* 2D **33**
Old Buckenham. *Norf* . . . 3D **17**
Oldeamere. *Cambs* 3A **14**
Old Felixstowe. *Suff* 3C **35**
Old Fletton. *Pet* 3C **13**
Old Hall Street. *Norf* 2C **11**
Old Hunstanton. *Norf* 1D **7**
Old Hurst. *Cambs* 2D **21**
Old Knebworth. *Herts* . . . 1D **37**
Old Leake. *Linc* 1B **6**
Old Newton. *Suff* 3D **25**
Old Somerby. *Linc* 2A **4**
Old Warden. *Beds* 2C **29**
Old Weston. *Cambs* 2B **20**
Olmstead Green.
Cambs 2D **31**
Olney. *Mil* 1A **28**
Onehouse. *Suff* 1D **33**
Ongar Hill. *Norf* 3C **7**
Onslow Green. *Essx* 2D **39**
Orford. *Suff* 2D **35**
Orlingbury. *Nptn* 2A **20**
Ormesby St Margaret.
Norf 1D **19**
Ormesby St Michael.
Norf 1D **19**
Orton Longueville.
Pet 3C **13**
Orton Waterville. *Pet* . . . 3C **13**
Orton Wistow. *Pet* 3C **13**
Orwell. *Cambs* 1A **30**
Osbournby. *Linc* 2B **4**
Ostend. *Essx* 3C **41**
Ostend. *Norf* 2C **11**
Otley. *Suff* 1B **34**
Oulton. *Norf* 3A **10**
Oulton. *Suff* 3D **19**
Oulton Broad. *Suff* 3D **19**
Oulton Street. *Norf* 3A **10**
Oundle. *Nptn* 1B **20**
Ousden. *Suff* 1A **32**
Outwell. *Norf* 2C **15**
Over. *Cambs* 2A **22**
Over End. *Cambs* 3B **12**
Overstrand. *Norf* 1B **10**
Ovington. *Essx* 2A **32**
Ovington. *Norf* 2C **17**
Oxborough. *Norf* 2A **16**
Oxen End. *Essx* 1D **39**
Oxley Green. *Essx* 2C **41**
Oxlode. *Cambs* 1B **22**
Oxwick. *Norf* 3C **9**

P

Pakefield. *Suff* 3D **19**
Pakenham. *Suff* 3C **25**
Palgrave. *Suff* 2A **26**
Pampisford. *Cambs* 2B **30**
Panfield. *Essx* 1A **40**
Panxworth. *Norf* 1C **19**
Papworth Everard.
Cambs 3D **21**
Papworth St Agnes.
Cambs 3D **21**
Parham. *Suff* 3C **27**
Parkeston. *Essx* 3B **34**
Park Street. *Herts* 3C **37**
Parsonage Green. *Essx* . . 2A **40**
Parson Drove. *Cambs* . . . 2A **14**
Passingford Bridge.
Essx 3C **39**
Paston. *Norf* 2C **11**
Patchetts Green. *Herts* . . 3C **37**
Patmore Heath. *Herts* . . . 1B **38**
Pattiswick. *Essx* 1B **40**
Pavenham. *Beds* 1A **28**
Peak Hill. *Linc* 1D **13**
Peakirk. *Pet* 2C **13**
Peaseland Green. *Norf* . . 1D **17**
Peasenhall. *Suff* 3C **27**
Peats Corner. *Suff* 3A **26**
Pebmarsh. *Essx* 3B **32**
Pegsdon. *Beds* 3C **29**
Peldon. *Essx* 2C **41**
Penn Street. *Buck* 3A **36**
Pennygate. *Norf* 3C **11**
Penny Hill. *Linc* 3A **6**
Pentlow. *Essx* 2B **32**
Pentney. *Norf* 1A **16**
Perry Green. *Essx* 1B **40**
Perry Green. *Herts* 2B **38**
Pertenhall. *Beds* 3B **20**
Peterborough. *Pet* . . . 3C **13** & **59**
Peter's Green. *Herts* 2C **37**
Petsoe End. *Mil* 2A **28**
Pettaugh. *Suff* 1A **34**
Pettistree. *Suff* 1B **34**
Pettywell. *Norf* 3D **9**
Piccadilly Corner. *Norf* . . 1B **26**
Piccotts End. *Herts* 3B **36**
Pickworth. *Linc* 2B **4**
Pickworth. *Rut* 1A **12**
Pidley. *Cambs* 2A **22**
Pilgrims Hatch. *Essx* 3C **39**
Pilsgate. *Pet* 2B **12**
Pilson Green. *Norf* 1C **19**
Pilton. *Nptn* 1B **20**
Pilton. *Rut* 2A **12**
Pinchbeck. *Linc* 3D **5**
Pinchbeck Bars. *Linc* 3C **5**
Pinchbeck West. *Linc* . . . 3D **5**
Pinford End. *Suff* 1B **32**
Pin Mill. *Suff* 3B **34**
Pirton. *Herts* 3C **29**
Pitstone. *Buck* 2A **36**
Pixey Green. *Suff* 2B **26**
Playford. *Suff* 2B **34**
Pledgdon Green. *Essx* . . . 1C **39**
Pleshey. *Essx* 2D **39**
Plumstead. *Norf* 2A **10**
Pode Hole. *Linc* 3D **5**
Podington. *Beds* 3A **20**
Point Clear. *Essx* 2D **41**
Pointon. *Linc* 2C **5**
Polebrook. *Nptn* 1B **20**
Pollard Street. *Norf* 2C **11**
Polstead. *Suff* 3C **33**
Polstead Heath. *Suff* . . . 2C **33**
Pondersbridge. *Cambs* . . 3D **13**
Pond Street. *Essx* 3B **30**
Pool Street. *Essx* 3A **32**
Poringland. *Norf* 2B **18**

Porter's Fen Corner.
Norf 2C **15**
Poslingford. *Suff* 2A **32**
Postwick. *Norf* 2B **18**
Potsgrove. *Beds* 1A **36**
Potten End. *Herts* 3B **36**
Pottergate Street. *Norf* . . 3A **18**
Potter Heigham. *Norf* . . . 1D **19**
Potters Bar. *Herts* 3D **37**
Potters Crouch. *Herts* . . . 3C **37**
Potter Street. *Essx* 3B **38**
Potthorpe. *Norf* 3C **9**
Potton. *Beds* 2D **29**
Pott Row. *Norf* 3A **8**
Poys Street. *Suff* 2C **27**
Poystreet Green. *Suff* . . . 1C **33**
Preston. *Herts* 1C **37**
Preston. *Rut* 2A **12**
Preston. *Suff* 1C **33**
Prestwood. *Buck* 3A **36**
Prickwillow. *Cambs* 1C **23**
Primrose Green. *Norf* . . . 1D **17**
Pristow Green. *Norf* 1A **26**
Puckeridge. *Herts* 1A **38**
Puddledock. *Norf* 3D **17**
Pulham Market. *Norf* . . . 1A **26**
Pulham St Mary. *Norf* . . . 1B **26**
Pulloxhill. *Beds* 3B **28**
Purleigh. *Essx* 3B **40**
Purl's Bridge. *Cambs* . . . 1B **22**
Puttenham. *Herts* 2A **36**
Puttock End. *Essx* 2B **32**
Puttock's End. *Essx* 2C **39**
Pye Corner. *Herts* 2B **38**
Pymore. *Cambs* 1B **22**
Pytchley. *Nptn* 2A **20**

Q

Quadring. *Linc* 2D **5**
Quadring Eaudike. *Linc* . . . 2D **5**
Quarrington. *Linc* 1B **4**
Queen Adelaide. *Cambs* . . . 1C **23**
Quendon. *Essx* 3C **31**
Quidenham. *Norf* 1D **25**

R

Rableyheath. *Herts* 2D **37**
Rackheath. *Norf* 1B **18**
Radlett. *Herts* 3C **37**
Radwell. *Beds* 1B **28**
Radwell. *Herts* 3D **29**
Radwinter. *Essx* 3D **31**
Rampton. *Cambs* 3B **22**
Ramsden Heath. *Essx* . . . 3A **40**
Ramsey. *Cambs* 1D **21**
Ramsey. *Essx* 3B **34**
Ramsey Forty Foot.
Cambs 1A **22**
Ramsey Heights.
Cambs 1D **21**
Ramsey Island. *Essx* 3C **41**
Ramsey Mereside.
Cambs 1D **21**
Ramsey St Mary's.
Cambs 1D **21**
Rank's Green. *Essx* 2A **40**
Ranworth. *Norf* 1C **19**
Rattlesden. *Suff* 1C **33**
Raunds. *Nptn* 2A **20**
Raveningham. *Norf* 3C **19**
Ravensden. *Beds* 1B **28**
Ravenstone. *Mil* 1A **28**
Raydon. *Suff* 3D **33**
Rayne. *Essx* 1A **40**
Reach. *Cambs* 3C **23**
Reading Green. *Suff* 2A **26**
Redbourn. *Herts* 2C **37**

Rede. *Suff* 1B **32**
Redenhall. *Norf* 1B **26**
Redgrave. *Suff* 2D **25**
Redhill. *Herts* 3D **29**
Redisham. *Suff* 1D **27**
Redlingfield. *Suff* 2A **26**
Red Lodge. *Suff* 2D **23**
Reed. *Herts* 3A **30**
Reed End. *Herts* 3A **30**
Reedham. *Norf* 2D **19**
Reepham. *Norf* 3D **9**
Rendham. *Suff* 3C **27**
Rendlesham. *Suff* 1C **35**
Renhold. *Beds* 1B **28**
Repps. *Norf* 1D **19**
Rettendon. *Essx* 3A **40**
Reydon. *Suff* 2D **27**
Reymerston. *Norf* 2D **17**
Rickinghall. *Suff* 2D **25**
Rickling. *Essx* 3B **30**
Rickling Green. *Essx* 1C **39**
Ridge. *Herts* 3D **37**
Ridgewell. *Essx* 2A **32**
Ridgmont. *Beds* 3A **28**
Ridlington. *Norf* 2C **11**
Ridlington. *Rut* 2A **12**
Ringland. *Norf* 1A **18**
Ring's End. *Cambs* 2A **14**
Ringsfield. *Suff* 1D **27**
Ringsfield Corner. *Suff* . . 1D **27**
Ringshall. *Buck* 2A **36**
Ringshall. *Suff* 1D **33**
Ringshall Stocks. *Suff* . . . 1D **33**
Ringstead. *Norf* 1A **8**
Ringstead. *Nptn* 2A **20**
Rippingale. *Linc* 3B **4**
Risby. *Suff* 3A **24**
Risegate. *Linc* 2D **5**
Riseley. *Beds* 3B **20**
Rishangles. *Suff* 3A **26**
Rivenhall. *Essx* 2B **40**
Rivenhall End. *Essx* 2B **40**
River Bank. *Cambs* 3C **23**
Road Green. *Norf* 3B **18**
Robinhood End. *Essx* . . . 3A **32**
Rockingham. *Nptn* 3A **12**
Rockland All Saints.
   Norf 3C **17**
Rockland St Mary. *Norf* . . 2C **19**
Rockland St Peter. *Norf* . . 3C **17**
Roe Green. *Herts* 3A **30**
Rogue's Alley. *Cambs* . . . 2A **14**
Rollesby. *Norf* 1D **19**
Rooksey Green. *Suff* 1C **33**
Rootham's Green. *Beds* . . 1C **29**
Ropsley. *Linc* 2A **4**
Rose Green. *Essx* 1B **40**
Rose Green. *Suff* 2C **33**
Rotten End. *Suff* 3C **27**
Rotten Row. *Norf* 1D **17**
Rougham. *Norf* 3B **8**
Rougham. *Suff* 3C **25**
Roughton. *Norf* 2B **10**
Roundbush Green.
   Essx 2C **39**
Row Green. *Essx* 1A **40**
Row Heath. *Essx* 2A **42**
Rowhedge. *Essx* 1D **41**
Rowsham. *Buck* 2A **36**
Roxton. *Beds* 1C **29**
Roxwell. *Essx* 3D **39**
Roydon. *Essx* 2B **38**
Roydon. *Norf* 1D **25**
         (nr. Diss)
Roydon. *Norf* 3A **8**
     (nr. King's Lynn)
Roydon Hamlet. *Essx* . . . 3B **38**
Royston. *Herts* 2A **30**
Rucklers Lane. *Herts* 3B **36**
Rudley Green. *Essx* 3B **40**
Rumburgh. *Suff* 1C **27**

Runcton Holme. *Norf* . . . 2D **15**
Runhall. *Norf* 2D **17**
Runham. *Norf* 1D **19**
Rushall. *Norf* 1A **26**
Rushbrooke. *Suff* 3B **24**
Rushden. *Herts* 3A **30**
Rushden. *Nptn* 3A **20**
Rushford. *Suff* 1C **25**
Rush Green. *Herts* 1D **37**
Rushmere. *Suff* 1D **27**
Rushmere St Andrew.
   Suff 2A **34**
Rushton. *Nptn* 1A **20**
Ruskington. *Linc* 1B **4**
Russel's Green. *Suff* 2B **26**
Ryhall. *Rut* 1B **12**

S

Sacombe. *Herts* 2A **38**
Saddle Bow. *Norf* 1D **15**
Saffron Walden. *Essx* . . . 3C **31**
Saham Hills. *Norf* 2C **17**
Saham Toney. *Norf* 2B **16**
St Albans. *Herts* 3C **37**
St Cross South Elmham.
   Suff 1B **26**
St Ippolyts. *Herts* 1C **37**
St Ives. *Cambs* 2A **22**
St James South Elmham.
   Suff 1C **27**
St John's Fen End. *Norf* . . 1C **15**
St Lawrence. *Essx* 3C **41**
St Leonards. *Buck* 3A **36**
St Margaret's. *Herts* 2B **36**
   (nr. Hemel Hempstead)
St Margarets. *Herts* 2A **38**
     (nr. Hoddesdon)
St Margaret South Elmham.
   Suff 1C **27**
St Michael South Elmham.
   Suff 1C **27**
St Neots. *Cambs* 3C **21**
St Nicholas South Elmham.
   Suff 1C **27**
St Olaves. *Norf* 3D **19**
St Osyth. *Essx* 2A **42**
St Osyth Heath. *Essx* . . . 2A **42**
St Paul's Walden. *Herts* . . 1C **37**
Salcott. *Essx* 2C **41**
Salford. *Beds* 3A **28**
Salhouse. *Norf* 1C **19**
Salle. *Norf* 3A **10**
Salph End. *Beds* 1B **28**
Saltby. *Leics* 3A **4**
Salters Lode. *Norf* 2C **15**
Salthouse. *Norf* 1D **9**
Sandhill. *Cambs* 1C **23**
Sandholme. *Linc* 2A **6**
Sandon. *Essx* 3A **40**
Sandon. *Herts* 3A **30**
Sandridge. *Herts* 2C **37**
Sandringham. *Norf* 3D **7**
Sandy. *Beds* 2C **29**
Santon Downham. *Suff* . . 1B **24**
Sapiston. *Suff* 2C **25**
Sapley. *Cambs* 2D **21**
Sapperton. *Linc* 2B **4**
Saracen's Head. *Linc* . . . 3A **6**
Sarratt. *Herts* 3B **36**
Sawbridgeworth. *Herts* . . 2B **38**
Sawston. *Cambs* 2B **30**
Sawtry. *Cambs* 1C **21**
Saxham Street. *Suff* 3D **25**
Saxlingham. *Norf* 2D **9**
Saxlingham Green. *Norf* . . 3B **18**
Saxlingham Nethergate.
   Norf 3B **18**
Saxlingham Thorpe.
   Norf 3B **18**

Saxmundham. *Suff* 3C **27**
Saxon Street. *Cambs* . . . 1D **31**
Saxtead. *Suff* 3B **26**
Saxtead Green. *Suff* 3B **26**
Saxthorpe. *Norf* 2A **10**
Scarning. *Norf* 1C **17**
School Green. *Essx* 3A **32**
Scole. *Norf* 2A **26**
Sco Ruston. *Norf* 3B **10**
Scottlethorpe. *Linc* 3B **4**
Scottow. *Norf* 3B **10**
Scoulton. *Norf* 2C **17**
Scrane End. *Linc* 1A **6**
Scratby. *Norf* 1D **19**
Scredington. *Linc* 1B **4**
Sculthorpe. *Norf* 2B **8**
Seadyke. *Linc* 2A **6**
Sea Palling. *Norf* 3D **11**
Seaton. *Rut* 3A **12**
Seawick. *Essx* 2A **42**
Sedgebrook. *Linc* 2A **4**
Sedgeford. *Norf* 2A **8**
Seething. *Norf* 3C **19**
Semer. *Suff* 2D **33**
Setchey. *Norf* 1D **15**
Sewards End. *Essx* 3C **31**
Sewardstone. *Essx* 3A **38**
Sewell. *Beds* 1A **36**
Sewstern. *Leics* 3A **4**
Shadingfield. *Suff* 1D **27**
Shadwell. *Norf* 1C **25**
Shalford. *Essx* 1A **40**
Shalford Green. *Essx* . . . 1A **40**
Sharnbrook. *Beds* 1A **28**
Sharpenhoe. *Beds* 3B **28**
Sharp Street. *Norf* 3C **11**
Sharrington. *Norf* 2D **9**
Sheering. *Essx* 2C **39**
Shefford. *Beds* 3C **29**
Shelfanger. *Norf* 1A **26**
Shelley. *Suff* 3D **33**
Shellow Bowells. *Essx* . . . 3D **39**
Shelton. *Beds* 3B **20**
Shelton. *Norf* 3B **18**
Shelton Green. *Norf* 3B **18**
Shenley. *Herts* 3C **37**
Shenleybury. *Herts* 3C **37**
Shepeau Stow. *Linc* 1A **14**
Shephall. *Herts* 1D **37**
Shepherds Gate. *Norf* . . . 1C **15**
Shepherd's Port. *Norf* . . . 2D **7**
Shepreth. *Cambs* 2A **30**
Shereford. *Norf* 3B **8**
Sheringham. *Norf* 1A **10**
Sherington. *Mil* 2A **28**
Shernborne. *Norf* 2A **8**
Shillington. *Beds* 3C **29**
Shimpling. *Norf* 1A **26**
Shimpling. *Suff* 1B **32**
Shimpling Street. *Suff* . . . 1B **32**
Shingay. *Cambs* 2A **30**
Shingham. *Norf* 2A **16**
Shingle Street. *Suff* 2C **35**
Shipdham. *Norf* 2C **17**
Shipmeadow. *Suff* 3C **19**
Shop Street. *Suff* 3B **26**
Short Green. *Norf* 1D **25**
Shortstown. *Beds* 2B **28**
Shotesham. *Norf* 3B **18**
Shotley. *Suff* 3B **34**
Shotley Gate. *Suff* 3B **34**
Shottisham. *Suff* 2C **35**
Shouldham. *Norf* 2D **15**
Shouldham Thorpe.
   Norf 2D **15**
Shropham. *Norf* 3C **17**
Shrub End. *Essx* 1C **41**
Shudy Camps. *Cambs* . . . 2D **31**
Sible Hedingham. *Essx* . . 3A **32**
Sibsey. *Linc* 1A **6**
Sibsey Fen Side. *Linc* . . . 1A **6**

Sibson. *Cambs* 3B **12**
Sibton. *Suff* 3C **27**
Sicklesmere. *Suff* 3B **24**
Sidestrand. *Norf* 2B **10**
Silfield. *Norf* 3A **18**
Silk Willoughby. *Linc* 1B **4**
Silsoe. *Beds* 3B **28**
Silver End. *Essx* 2B **40**
Silvergate. *Norf* 3A **10**
Silverley's Green. *Suff* . . . 2B **26**
Six Mile Bottom.
   Cambs 1C **31**
Sizewell. *Suff* 3D **27**
Skeldyke. *Linc* 2A **6**
Skeyton. *Norf* 3B **10**
Skeyton Corner. *Norf* . . . 3B **10**
Skillington. *Linc* 3A **4**
Skirbeck. *Linc* 1A **6**
Skirbeck Quarter. *Linc* . . . 1A **6**
Skye Green. *Essx* 1B **40**
Slade Field. *Cambs* 1A **22**
Slapton. *Buck* 1A **36**
Sleaford. *Linc* 1B **4**
Slip End. *Beds* 2B **36**
Slipton. *Nptn* 2A **20**
Sloley. *Norf* 3B **10**
Smallburgh. *Norf* 3C **11**
Smallworth. *Norf* 1D **25**
Smeeth, The. *Norf* 1C **15**
Smith's Green. *Essx* 1C **39**
Smithwood Green. *Suff* . . . 1C **33**
Smyth's Green. *Essx* 2C **41**
Snailwell. *Cambs* 3D **23**
Snape. *Suff* 1C **35**
Snetterton. *Norf* 3C **17**
Snettisham. *Norf* 2D **7**
Snow Street. *Norf* 1D **25**
Soham. *Cambs* 2C **23**
Soham Cotes. *Cambs* . . . 2C **23**
Somerleyton. *Suff* 3D **19**
Somersham. *Cambs* 2C **21**
Somersham. *Suff* 2D **33**
Somerton. *Suff* 1B **32**
Sotterley. *Suff* 1D **27**
Soulbury. *Buck* 1A **36**
Souldrop. *Beds* 3A **20**
South Acre. *Norf* 1B **16**
Southburgh. *Norf* 2C **17**
South Burlingham.
   Norf 2C **19**
South Cove. *Suff* 1D **27**
South Creake. *Norf* 2B **8**
Southery. *Norf* 3D **15**
Southey Green. *Essx* 3A **32**
Southgate. *Norf* 3A **10**
      (nr. Aylsham)
Southgate. *Norf* 2B **8**
     (nr. Fakenham)
South Green. *Essx* 2D **41**
South Hanningfield.
   Essx 3A **40**
South Heath. *Buck* 3A **36**
South Heath. *Essx* 2A **42**
Southill. *Beds* 2C **29**
South Kyme. *Linc* 1C **5**
South Lopham. *Norf* 1D **25**
South Luffenham. *Rut* . . . 2A **12**
South Mimms. *Herts* 3D **37**
Southminster. *Essx* 3C **41**
Southoe. *Cambs* 3C **21**
Southolt. *Suff* 3A **26**
Southorpe. *Pet* 2B **12**
South Pickenham. *Norf* . . 2B **16**
South Rauceby. *Linc* 1B **4**
South Raynham. *Norf* 3B **8**
Southrepps. *Norf* 2B **10**
South Runcton. *Norf* 2D **15**
Southtown. *Norf* 2D **19**
South Walsham. *Norf* . . . 1C **19**
Southwick. *Nptn* 3B **12**
South Witham. *Linc* 1A **12**

Southwold. *Suff* 2D **27**
Southwood. *Norf* 2C **19**
South Woodham Ferrers.
　Essx 3B **40**
South Wootton. *Norf* 3D **7**
Sowley Green. *Suff* 1A **32**
Spa Common. *Norf* 2B **10**
Spalding. *Linc* 3D **5**
Spaldwick. *Cambs* 2C **21**
Spanby. *Linc* 2B **4**
Sparham. *Norf* 1D **17**
Sparhamhill. *Norf* 1D **17**
Sparrow Green. *Norf* 1C **17**
Speen. *Buck* 3A **36**
Spellbrook. *Herts* 2B **38**
Spexhall. *Suff* 1C **27**
Spixworth. *Norf* 1B **18**
Spooner Row. *Norf* 3D **17**
Sporle. *Norf* 1B **16**
Sproughton. *Suff* 2A **34**
Sprowston. *Norf* 1B **18**
Sproxton. *Leics* 3A **4**
Stacksford. *Norf* 3D **17**
Stagden Cross. *Essx* 2D **39**
Stagsden. *Beds* 2A **28**
Stainby. *Linc* 3A **4**
Stainfield. *Linc* 3B **4**
Stalham. *Norf* 3C **11**
Stalham Green. *Norf* 3C **11**
Stambourne. *Essx* 3A **32**
Stamford. *Linc* 2B **12**
Stanborough. *Herts* 2D **37**
Stanbridge. *Beds* 1A **36**
Standon. *Herts* 1A **38**
Standon Green End.
　Herts 2A **38**
Standwell Green. *Suff* . . . 2A **26**
Stanfield. *Norf* 3C **9**
Stanford. *Beds* 2C **29**
Stanford Rivers. *Essx* . . . 3C **39**
Stanground. *Pet* 3D **13**
Stanhoe. *Norf* 2B **8**
Stanion. *Nptn* 1A **20**
Stanningfield. *Suff* 1B **32**
Stansfield. *Suff* 1A **32**
Stanstead. *Suff* 2B **32**
Stanstead Abbotts.
　Herts 2A **38**
Stansted (London) Airport.
　Essx 1C **39**
Stansted Mountfitchet.
　Essx 1C **39**
Stanton. *Suff* 2C **25**
Stanton Chare. *Suff* 2C **25**
Stanton Street. *Suff* 3C **25**
Stanway. *Essx* 1C **41**
Stanwick. *Nptn* 2A **20**
Stapleford. *Cambs* 1B **30**
Stapleford. *Herts* 2A **38**
Stapleford Tawney.
　Essx 3C **39**
Staploe. *Beds* 3C **21**
Starling's Green. *Essx* . . . 3B **30**
Starston. *Norf* 1B **26**
Start Hill. *Essx* 1C **39**
Staughton Green.
　Cambs 3C **21**
Staughton Highway.
　Cambs 3C **21**
Stebbing. *Essx* 1D **39**
Stebbing Green. *Essx* . . . 1D **39**
Steeple. *Essx* 3C **41**
Steeple Bumpstead.
　Essx 2D **31**
Steeple Gidding.
　Cambs 1C **21**
Steeple Morden.
　Cambs 2D **29**
Steppingley. *Beds* 3B **28**
Sternfield. *Suff* 3C **27**
Stetchworth. *Cambs* 1D **31**

Stevenage. *Herts* 1D **37**
Stevington. *Beds* 1A **28**
Stevington End. *Cambs* . . . 2D **31**
Stewartby. *Beds* 2B **28**
Stewkley. *Buck* 1A **36**
Stibbard. *Norf* 3C **9**
Stibbington. *Cambs* 3B **12**
Stickling Green. *Essx* 3B **30**
Stiffkey. *Norf* 1C **9**
Stilton. *Cambs* 1C **21**
Stisted. *Essx* 1A **40**
Stock. *Essx* 3D **39**
Stocking Green. *Essx* . . . 3C **31**
Stocking Pelham. *Herts* . . 1B **38**
Stockstreet. *Essx* 1B **40**
Stockton. *Norf* 3C **19**
Stody. *Norf* 2D **9**
Stoke Ash. *Suff* 2A **26**
Stoke by Clare. *Suff* 2A **32**
Stoke-by-Nayland. *Suff* . . 3C **33**
Stoke Doyle. *Nptn* 1B **20**
Stoke Dry. *Rut* 3A **12**
Stoke Ferry. *Norf* 3A **16**
Stoke Hammond. *Buck* . . 1A **36**
Stoke Holy Cross. *Norf* . . 2B **18**
Stoke Rochford. *Linc* 3A **4**
Stokesby. *Norf* 1D **19**
Stondon Massey. *Essx* . . 3C **39**
Stonea. *Cambs* 3B **14**
Stone Bridge Corner.
　Pet 2D **13**
Stonely. *Cambs* 3C **21**
Stones Green. *Essx* 1A **42**
Stone Street. *Suff* 3C **33**
　　　　　　　　　(nr. Boxford)
Stone Street. *Suff* 1C **27**
　　　　　　　　(nr. Halesworth)
Stoneyhills. *Essx* 3C **41**
Stonham Aspal. *Suff* 1A **34**
Stopsley. *Lutn* 1C **37**
Stotfold. *Beds* 3D **29**
Stoven. *Suff* 1D **27**
Stow. *Linc* 2B **4**
Stow Bardolph. *Norf* 2D **15**
Stow Bedon. *Norf* 3C **17**
Stowbridge. *Norf* 2D **15**
Stow cum Quy. *Cambs* . . 3C **23**
Stowlangtoft. *Suff* 3C **25**
Stow Longa. *Cambs* 2C **21**
Stow Maries. *Essx* 3B **40**
Stowmarket. *Suff* 1D **33**
Stowupland. *Suff* 1D **33**
Stradbroke. *Suff* 2B **26**
Stradishall. *Suff* 1A **32**
Stradsett. *Norf* 2D **15**
Stragglethorpe. *Linc* 1A **4**
Stratford St Andrew.
　Suff 3C **27**
Stratford St Mary. *Suff* . . 3D **33**
Stratton St Michael.
　Norf 3B **18**
Stratton Strawless.
　Norf 3B **10**
Streatley. *Beds* 1B **36**
Streetly End. *Cambs* 2D **31**
Strethall. *Essx* 3B **30**
Stretham. *Cambs* 2C **23**
Stretton. *Rut* 1A **12**
Strixton. *Nptn* 3A **20**
Stroxton. *Linc* 2A **4**
Strugg's Hill. *Linc* 2D **5**
Strumpshaw. *Norf* 2C **19**
Stubbs Green. *Norf* 3C **19**
Stubton. *Linc* 1A **4**
Studham. *Beds* 2B **36**
Stuntney. *Cambs* 2C **23**
Sturmer. *Essx* 2D **31**
Stuston. *Suff* 2A **26**
Stutton. *Suff* 3A **34**
Sudborough. *Nptn* 1A **20**
Sudbourne. *Suff* 1D **35**

Sudbrook. *Linc* 1A **4**
Sudbury. *Suff* 2B **32**
Suffield. *Norf* 2B **10**
Summerfield. *Norf* 2A **8**
Sundon Park. *Lutn* 1B **36**
Surfleet. *Linc* 3D **5**
Surfleet Seas End. *Linc* . . 3D **5**
Surlingham. *Norf* 2C **19**
Surrex. *Essx* 1B **40**
Sustead. *Norf* 2A **10**
Suton. *Norf* 3D **17**
Sutterton. *Linc* 2D **5**
Sutterton Dowdyke.
　Linc 2D **5**
Sutton. *Beds* 2D **29**
Sutton. *Cambs* 2B **22**
Sutton. *Norf* 3C **11**
Sutton. *Pet* 3B **12**
Sutton. *Suff* 2C **35**
Sutton Bridge. *Linc* 3B **6**
Sutton Corner. *Linc* 3B **6**
Sutton Crosses. *Linc* 3B **6**
Sutton Gault. *Cambs* 2B **22**
Sutton St Edmund.
　Linc 1A **14**
Sutton St Edmund's Common.
　Linc 2A **14**
Sutton St James. *Linc* . . . 1A **14**
Swaffham. *Norf* 2B **16**
Swaffham Bulbeck.
　Cambs 3C **23**
Swaffham Prior.
　Cambs 3C **23**
Swafield. *Norf* 2B **10**
Swainsthorpe. *Norf* 2B **18**
Swannington. *Norf* 1A **18**
Swan Street. *Essx* 1B **40**
Swanton Abbot. *Norf* 3B **10**
Swanton Morley. *Norf* . . . 1D **17**
Swanton Novers. *Norf* . . . 2D **9**
Swarby. *Linc* 1B **4**
Swardeston. *Norf* 2B **18**
Swaton. *Linc* 2C **5**
Swavesey. *Cambs* 3A **22**
Swayfield. *Linc* 3A **4**
Swefling. *Suff* 3C **27**
Swilland. *Suff* 1A **34**
Swineshead. *Beds* 3B **20**
Swineshead. *Linc* 1D **5**
Swineshead Bridge. *Linc* . . 1D **5**
Swingbrow. *Cambs* 1A **22**
Swingleton Green. *Suff* . . 2C **33**
Swinstead. *Linc* 3B **4**
Syderstone. *Norf* 2B **8**
Syleham. *Suff* 2B **26**
Syston. *Linc* 1A **4**

T

Tacolneston. *Norf* 3A **18**
Tadlow. *Cambs* 2D **29**
Takeley. *Essx* 1C **39**
Takeley Street. *Essx* 1C **39**
Tallington. *Linc* 2B **12**
Tamworth Green. *Linc* . . . 1A **6**
Tannington. *Suff* 3B **26**
Tan Office Green. *Suff* . . . 1A **32**
Tansor. *Nptn* 3B **12**
Tasburgh. *Norf* 3B **18**
Tatterford. *Norf* 3B **8**
Tattersett. *Norf* 2B **8**
Tattingstone. *Suff* 3A **34**
Tattingstone White Horse.
　Suff 3A **34**
Taverham. *Norf* 1A **18**
Taverners Green. *Essx* . . 2C **39**
Tebworth. *Beds* 1A **36**
Teigh. *Rut* 1A **12**
Tempsford. *Beds* 1C **29**
Tendring. *Essx* 1A **42**

Tendring Green. *Essx* . . . 1A **42**
Ten Mile Bank. *Norf* 3D **15**
Terling. *Essx* 2A **40**
Terrick. *Buck* 3A **36**
Terrington St Clement.
　Norf 3C **7**
Terrington St John.
　Norf 1C **15**
Teversham. *Cambs* 1B **30**
Tewin. *Herts* 2D **37**
Tharston. *Norf* 3A **18**
Thaxted. *Essx* 3D **31**
Theberton. *Suff* 3D **27**
Thelnetham. *Suff* 2D **25**
Thelveton. *Norf* 1A **26**
Themelthorpe. *Norf* 3D **9**
Therfield. *Herts* 3A **30**
Thetford. *Linc* 1C **13**
Thetford. *Norf* 1B **24**
Theydon Bois. *Essx* 3B **38**
Thistleton. *Rut* 1A **12**
Thistley Green. *Suff* 2D **23**
Tholomas Drove.
　Cambs 2B **14**
Thompson. *Norf* 3C **17**
Thorington. *Suff* 2D **27**
Thorington Street. *Suff* . . 3D **33**
Thorley. *Herts* 2B **38**
Thorley Street. *Herts* 2B **38**
Thornage. *Norf* 2D **9**
Thorncote Green. *Beds* . . 2C **29**
Thorndon. *Suff* 3A **26**
Thorney. *Pet* 2D **13**
Thorney Toll. *Cambs* 2A **14**
Thornham. *Norf* 1A **8**
Thornham Magna. *Suff* . . 2A **26**
Thornham Parva. *Suff* . . . 2A **26**
Thornhaugh. *Pet* 2B **12**
Thorns. *Suff* 1A **32**
Thornwood Common.
　Essx 3B **38**
Thorpe. *Norf* 3D **19**
Thorpe Abbotts. *Norf* . . . 2A **26**
Thorpe by Water. *Rut* . . . 3A **12**
Thorpe Common. *Suff* . . . 3B **34**
Thorpe End. *Norf* 1B **18**
Thorpe Green. *Essx* 1A **42**
Thorpe Green. *Suff* 1C **33**
Thorpe Hamlet. *Norf* 2B **18**
Thorpe Latimer. *Linc* 1C **5**
Thorpe-le-Soken. *Essx* . . 1A **42**
Thorpe Market. *Norf* 2B **10**
Thorpe Marriott. *Norf* . . . 1A **18**
Thorpe Morieux. *Suff* . . . 1C **33**
Thorpeness. *Suff* 3D **27**
Thorpe St Andrew.
　Norf 2B **18**
Thorpe Waterville.
　Nptn 1B **20**
Thorpland. *Norf* 2D **15**
Thorrington. *Essx* 1D **41**
Thrandeston. *Suff* 2A **26**
Thrapston. *Nptn* 2A **20**
Three Holes. *Norf* 2C **15**
Threekingham. *Linc* 2B **4**
Thrigby. *Norf* 1D **19**
Thriplow. *Cambs* 2B **30**
Throckenholt. *Linc* 2A **14**
Throcking. *Herts* 3A **30**
Thundridge. *Herts* 2A **38**
Thurgarton. *Norf* 2A **10**
Thurlby. *Linc* 1C **13**
Thurleigh. *Beds* 1B **28**
Thurlton. *Norf* 3D **19**
Thurne. *Norf* 1D **19**
Thurning. *Norf* 3D **9**
Thurning. *Nptn* 1B **20**
Thursford. *Norf* 2C **9**
Thursford Green. *Norf* . . . 2C **9**
Thurston. *Suff* 3C **25**
Thurston End. *Suff* 1A **32**

Thurton. *Norf* 2C **19**
Thuxton. *Norf* 2D **17**
Thwaite. *Suff* 3A **26**
Thwaite St Mary. *Norf* . . . 3C **19**
Tibenham. *Norf* 1A **26**
Tickencote. *Rut* 2A **12**
Tilbrook. *Cambs* 3B **20**
Tilbury Green. *Essx* 2A **32**
Tilbury Juxta Clare.
   Essx 2A **32**
Tillingham. *Essx* 3C **41**
Tilney All Saints. *Norf* . . . 1C **15**
Tilney Fen Side. *Norf* 1C **15**
Tilney High End. *Norf* 1C **15**
Tilney St Lawrence.
   Norf 1C **15**
Tilsworth. *Beds* 1A **36**
Timworth Green. *Suff* 3B **24**
Tingrith. *Beds* 3B **28**
Tinwell. *Rut* 2B **12**
Tips End. *Cambs* 3C **15**
Tiptree. *Essx* 2B **40**
Tiptree Heath. *Essx* 2B **40**
Titchmarsh. *Nptn* 2B **20**
Titchwell. *Norf* 1A **8**
Tittleshall. *Norf* 3B **8**
Tivetshall St Margaret.
   Norf 1A **26**
Tivetshall St Mary.
   Norf 1A **26**
Tixover. *Rut* 2A **12**
Toddington. *Beds* 1B **36**
Toft. *Cambs* 1A **30**
Toft. *Linc* 1B **12**
Toft Monks. *Norf* 3D **19**
Toftrees. *Norf* 3B **8**
Toftwood. *Norf* 1C **17**
Tollesbury. *Essx* 2C **41**
Tolleshunt D'Arcy. *Essx* . . . 2C **41**
Tolleshunt Knights.
   Essx 2C **41**
Tolleshunt Major. *Essx* . . . 2C **41**
Tonwell. *Herts* 2A **38**
Toot Hill. *Essx* 3C **39**
Topcroft. *Norf* 3B **18**
Topcroft Street. *Norf* 3B **18**
Toppesfield. *Essx* 3A **32**
Toprow. *Norf* 3A **18**
Toseland. *Cambs* 3D **21**
Tostock. *Suff* 3C **25**
Tottenhill. *Norf* 1D **15**
Tottenhill Row. *Norf* 1D **15**
Totternhoe. *Beds* 1A **36**
Tower End. *Norf* 1D **15**
Town End. *Cambs* 3B **14**
Towngate. *Linc* 1C **13**
Townsend. *Herts* 3C **37**
Town Street. *Suff* 1A **24**
Trimingham. *Norf* 2B **10**
Trimley Lower Street.
   Suff 3B **34**
Trimley St Martin. *Suff* . . . 3B **34**
Trimley St Mary. *Suff* 3B **34**
Tring. *Herts* 2A **36**
Troston. *Suff* 2B **24**
Trowley Bottom. *Herts* . . . 2B **36**
Trowse Newton. *Norf* 2B **18**
Trumpington. *Cambs* 1B **30**
Trunch. *Norf* 2B **10**
Tuddenham. *Suff* 2A **34**
            (nr. Ipswich)
Tuddenham. *Suff* 2A **24**
          (nr. Mildenhall)
Tumbler's Green. *Essx* 1B **40**
Tungate. *Norf* 3B **10**
Tunstall. *Norf* 2D **19**
Tunstall. *Suff* 1C **35**
Tunstead. *Norf* 3B **10**
Turnford. *Herts* 3A **38**
Turvey. *Beds* 1A **28**
Tuttington. *Norf* 3B **10**

Twenty. *Linc* 3C **5**
Twinstead. *Essx* 3B **32**
Twinstead Green. *Essx* . . . 3B **32**
Twyford. *Norf* 3D **9**
Twywell. *Nptn* 2A **20**
Tyby. *Norf* 3D **9**
Tydd Gote. *Linc* 1B **14**
Tydd St Giles. *Cambs* 1B **14**
Tydd St Mary. *Linc* 1B **14**
Tye Green. *Essx* 1C **39**
     (nr. Bishop's Stortford)
Tye Green. *Essx* 1A **40**
          (nr. Braintree)
Tye Green. *Essx* 3C **31**
     (nr. Saffron Walden)
Tyler's Green. *Essx* 3C **39**
Tyringham. *Mil* 2A **28**

U

Ubbeston Green. *Suff* . . . 2C **27**
Uffington. *Linc* 2B **12**
Ufford. *Pet* 2B **12**
Ufford. *Suff* 1B **34**
Uggeshall. *Suff* 1D **27**
Ugley. *Essx* 1C **39**
Ugley Green. *Essx* 1C **39**
Ulting. *Essx* 3B **40**
Undley. *Suff* 1D **23**
Upend. *Cambs* 1A **32**
Upgate. *Norf* 1A **18**
Upgate Street. *Norf* 3D **17**
Upper Benefield. *Nptn* 1A **20**
Upper Caldecote. *Beds* . . . 2C **29**
Upper Dean. *Beds* 3B **20**
Upper Dovercourt.
   Essx 3B **34**
Upper Dunsley. *Herts* 2A **36**
Upper Gravenhurst.
   Beds 3C **29**
Upper Green. *Essx* 3B **30**
Upper Hambleton. *Rut* . . . 2A **12**
Upper Hellesdon. *Norf* . . . 1B **18**
Upper Layham. *Suff* 2D **33**
Upper North Dean.
   Buck 3A **36**
Upper Shelton. *Beds* 2A **28**
Upper Sheringham.
   Norf 1A **10**
Upper Staploe. *Beds* 1C **29**
Upper Stoke. *Norf* 2B **18**
Upper Stondon. *Beds* 3C **29**
Upper Street. *Norf* 1C **19**
         (nr. Horning)
Upper Street. *Norf* 1C **19**
        (nr. Hoveton)
Upper Street. *Suff* 3A **34**
Upper Sundon. *Beds* 1B **36**
Uppingham. *Rut* 3A **12**
Upshire. *Essx* 3B **38**
Upthorpe. *Suff* 2C **25**
Upton. *Cambs* 2C **21**
Upton. *Norf* 1C **19**
Upton. *Pet* 2C **13**
Upton End. *Beds* 3C **29**
Upware. *Cambs* 2C **23**
Upwell. *Cambs* 2B **14**
Upwick Green. *Herts* 1B **38**
Upwood. *Cambs* 1D **21**

W

Wacton. *Norf* 3A **18**
Wadenhoe. *Nptn* 1B **20**
Wadesmill. *Herts* 2A **38**
Wakerley. *Nptn* 3A **12**
Wakes Colne. *Essx* 1B **40**
Walberswick. *Suff* 2D **27**
Walcot. *Linc* 2B **4**

Walcot Green. *Norf* 1A **26**
Walcott. *Norf* 2C **11**
Waldringfield. *Suff* 2B **34**
Walkern. *Herts* 1D **37**
Wallington. *Herts* 3D **29**
Walpole. *Suff* 2C **27**
Walpole Cross Keys.
   Norf 1C **15**
Walpole Gate. *Norf* 1C **15**
Walpole Highway. *Norf* . . . 1C **15**
Walpolelane. *Suff* 2C **27**
Walpole Marsh. *Norf* 1B **14**
Walpole St Andrew.
   Norf 1C **15**
Walpole St Peter. *Norf* 1C **15**
Walsham le Willows.
   Suff 2D **25**
Walsoken. *Cambs* 1B **14**
Walsworth. *Herts* 3C **29**
Waltham Abbey. *Essx* . . . 3A **38**
Waltham Cross. *Herts* 3A **38**
Waltham's Cross. *Essx* . . . 3D **31**
Walton. *Mil* 3A **28**
Walton. *Pet* 2C **13**
Walton. *Suff* 3B **34**
Walton Highway. *Norf* 1B **14**
Walton-on-the-Naze.
   Essx 1B **42**
Wangford. *Suff* 1A **24**
      (nr. Lakenheath)
Wangford. *Suff* 2D **27**
      (nr. Southwold)
Wansford. *Pet* 3B **12**
Warboys. *Cambs* 1A **22**
Ward Green. *Suff* 3D **25**
Wardhedges. *Beds* 3B **28**
Wardy Hill. *Cambs* 1B **22**
Ware. *Herts* 2A **38**
Wareside. *Herts* 2A **38**
Waresley. *Cambs* 1D **29**
Wargate. *Linc* 2D **5**
Warham. *Norf* 1C **9**
Warkton. *Nptn* 2A **20**
Warmington. *Nptn* 3B **12**
Warners End. *Herts* 3B **36**
Warrington. *Mil* 1A **28**
Washbrook. *Suff* 2A **34**
Waterbeach. *Cambs* 3B **22**
Waterden. *Norf* 2B **8**
Water End. *Beds* 3B **28**
Water End. *Herts* 3D **37**
        (nr. Hatfield)
Water End. *Herts* 2B **36**
    (nr. Hemel Hempstead)
Waterford. *Herts* 2A **38**
Waterloo. *Norf* 1B **18**
Water Newton. *Cambs* . . . 3C **13**
Waterside. *Buck* 3A **36**
Waterside. *Cambs* 2D **23**
Watford. *Herts* 3B **36**
Watlington. *Norf* 1D **15**
Wattisfield. *Suff* 2D **25**
Wattisham. *Suff* 1D **33**
Watton. *Norf* 2C **17**
Watton at Stone. *Herts* . . . 2D **37**
Wavendon. *Mil* 3A **28**
Waxham. *Norf* 3D **11**
Way Head. *Cambs* 1B **22**
Weasenham All Saints.
   Norf 3B **8**
Weasenham St Peter.
   Norf 3B **8**
Weekley. *Nptn* 1A **20**
Weeley. *Essx* 1A **42**
Weeley Heath. *Essx* 1A **42**
Weeting. *Norf* 1A **24**
Welborne. *Norf* 1D **17**
Welby. *Linc* 2A **4**
Welches Dam. *Cambs* 1B **22**
Weldon. *Nptn* 1A **20**
Welham Green. *Herts* 3D **37**

Wellingborough. *Nptn* . . . 3A **20**
Wellingham. *Norf* 3B **8**
Wellpond Green. *Herts* . . . 1B **38**
Wells-next-the-Sea. *Norf* . . . 1C **9**
Welney. *Norf* 3C **15**
Welwyn. *Herts* 2D **37**
Welwyn Garden City.
   Herts 2D **37**
Wendens Ambo. *Essx* 3C **31**
Wending. *Norf* 1C **17**
Wendover. *Buck* 3A **36**
Wendy. *Cambs* 2A **30**
Wenhaston. *Suff* 2D **27**
Wennington. *Cambs* 2D **21**
Wentworth. *Cambs* 2B **22**
Wereham. *Norf* 2D **15**
Werrington. *Pet* 2C **13**
West Acre. *Norf* 1A **16**
West Barsham. *Norf* 2C **9**
West Beckham. *Norf* 2A **10**
West Bergholt. *Essx* 1C **41**
West Bilney. *Norf* 1A **16**
Westborough. *Linc* 1A **4**
West Briggs. *Norf* 1D **15**
Westby. *Linc* 3A **4**
West Caister. *Norf* 1D **19**
West Deeping. *Linc* 2C **13**
West Dereham. *Norf* 2D **15**
West End. *Beds* 1A **28**
West End. *Cambs* 3B **14**
West End. *Herts* 3D **37**
West End. *Linc* 1A **6**
West End. *Norf* 1D **19**
Westerfield. *Suff* 2A **34**
Westfield. *Norf* 2C **17**
Westgate. *Norf* 1C **9**
Westhall. *Suff* 1D **27**
West Hanningfield.
   Essx 3A **40**
West Head. *Norf* 2C **15**
Westhorpe. *Linc* 2D **5**
Westhorpe. *Suff* 3D **25**
West Leith. *Buck* 2A **36**
Westleton. *Suff* 3D **27**
West Lexham. *Norf* 1B **16**
Westley. *Suff* 3B **24**
Westley Waterless.
   Cambs 1D **31**
West Lynn. *Norf* 1D **15**
West Mersea. *Essx* 2D **41**
Westmill. *Herts* 1A **38**
     (nr. Buntingford)
Westmill. *Herts* 3C **29**
       (nr. Hitchin)
West Newton. *Norf* 3D **7**
Weston. *Herts* 3D **29**
Weston. *Linc* 3D **5**
Weston. *Suff* 1D **27**
Weston Colville.
   Cambs 1D **31**
Weston Ditch. *Suff* 2D **23**
Weston Green. *Cambs* 1D **31**
Weston Green. *Norf* 1A **18**
Weston Hills. *Linc* 1D **13**
Westoning. *Beds* 3B **28**
Weston Longville. *Norf* . . . 1A **18**
Weston Turville. *Buck* 2A **36**
Weston Underwood.
   Mil 1A **28**
West Perry. *Cambs* 3C **21**
West Poringland. *Norf* 2B **18**
West Raynham. *Norf* 3B **8**
West Row. *Suff* 2D **23**
West Rudham. *Norf* 3B **8**
West Runton. *Norf* 1A **10**
Westry. *Cambs* 3A **14**
West Somerton. *Norf* 1D **19**
West Stow. *Suff* 2B **24**
West Tofts. *Norf* 3B **16**
West Walton. *Norf* 1B **14**
Westwick. *Cambs* 3B **22**

Westwick. *Norf* 3B **10**
West Wickham. *Cambs* . . . 2D **31**
West Willoughby. *Linc* 1A **4**
West Winch. *Norf* 1D **15**
Westwood. *Pet* 3C **13**
West Wratting. *Cambs* . . . 1D **31**
Wetherden. *Suff* 3D **25**
Wetheringsett. *Suff* 3A **26**
Wethersfield. *Essx* 3A **32**
Wetherup Street. *Suff* . . . 3A **26**
Weybourne. *Norf* 1A **10**
Weybread. *Suff* 1B **26**
Whaddon. *Cambs* 2A **30**
Whaplode. *Linc* 3A **6**
Whaplode Drove. *Linc* . . . 1A **14**
Whaplode St Catherine.
    Linc 3A **6**
Wharley End. *Beds* 2A **28**
Whatfield. *Suff* 2D **33**
Wheatacre. *Norf* 3D **19**
Wheathampstead.
    Herts 2C **37**
Whelpley Hill. *Buck* 3A **36**
Whepstead. *Suff* 1B **32**
Wherstead. *Suff* 2A **34**
Whimpwell Green. *Norf* . . 3C **11**
Whinburgh. *Norf* 2D **17**
Whipsnade. *Beds* 2B **36**
Whissonsett. *Norf* 3C **9**
Whiston. *Nptn* 3A **20**
Whiteash Green. *Essx* . . . 3A **32**
White Colne. *Essx* 1B **40**
White Horse Common.
    Norf 3C **11**
White Notley. *Essx* 2A **40**
White Roding. *Essx* 2C **39**
Whitestreet Green. *Suff* . . 3C **33**
Whitington. *Norf* 3A **16**
Whittlesey. *Cambs* 3D **13**
Whittlesford. *Cambs* 2B **30**
Whitwell. *Herts* 1C **37**
Whitwell. *Rut* 2A **12**
Wicken. *Cambs* 2C **23**
Wicken Bonhunt. *Essx* . . 3B **30**
Wicken Green Village.
    Norf 2B **8**
Wicker Street Green.
    Suff 2C **33**
Wickham Bishops.
    Essx 2B **40**
Wickhambrook. *Suff* 1A **32**
Wickham Green. *Suff* . . . 3D **25**
Wickham Market. *Suff* . . . 1C **35**
Wickhampton. *Norf* 2D **19**
Wickham St Paul. *Essx* . . . 3B **32**

Wickham Skeith. *Suff* 3D **25**
Wickham Street. *Suff* 3D **25**
Wicklewood. *Norf* 2D **17**
Wickmere. *Norf* 2A **10**
Widdington. *Essx* 3C **31**
Widford. *Essx* 3D **39**
Widford. *Herts* 2B **38**
Widmer End. *Buck* 3A **36**
Wiggenhall St Germans.
    Norf 1C **15**
Wiggenhall St Mary Magdalen.
    Norf 1C **15**
Wiggenhall St Mary the Virgin.
    Norf 1C **15**
Wiggenhall St Peter.
    Norf 1D **15**
Wiggens Green. *Essx* 2D **31**
Wigginton. *Herts* 2A **36**
Wighton. *Norf* 1C **9**
Wigsthorpe. *Nptn* 1B **20**
Wigtoft. *Linc* 2D **5**
Wilburton. *Cambs* 2B **22**
Wilby. *Norf* 1D **25**
Wilby. *Nptn* 3A **20**
Wilby. *Suff* 2B **26**
Wilden. *Beds* 1B **28**
Wilde Street. *Suff* 2A **24**
Willen. *Mil* 2A **28**
Willian. *Herts* 3D **29**
Willingale. *Essx* 3C **39**
Willingham. *Cambs* 2B **22**
Willingham Green.
    Cambs 1D **31**
Willington. *Beds* 2C **29**
Willisham Tye. *Suff* 1D **33**
Willows Green. *Essx* 2A **40**
Wilney Green. *Norf* 1D **25**
Wilsford. *Linc* 1B **4**
Wilstead. *Beds* 2B **28**
Wilsthorpe. *Linc* 1B **12**
Wilstone. *Herts* 2A **36**
Wimbish. *Essx* 3C **31**
Wimbish Green. *Essx* 3D **31**
Wimblington. *Cambs* 3B **14**
Wimbotsham. *Norf* 2D **15**
Windsor Green. *Suff* 1B **32**
Winfarthing. *Norf* 1A **26**
Wing. *Buck* 1A **36**
Wing. *Rut* 2A **12**
Wingfield. *Beds* 1B **36**
Wingfield. *Suff* 2B **26**
Wingrave. *Buck* 2A **36**
Winston. *Suff* 3A **26**
Winterton-on-Sea.
    Norf 1D **19**

Winwick. *Cambs* 1C **21**
Wisbech. *Cambs* 1B **14**
Wisbech St Mary.
    Cambs 2B **14**
Wissett. *Suff* 2C **27**
Wistow. *Cambs* 1D **21**
Witcham. *Cambs* 1B **22**
Witchford. *Cambs* 2C **23**
Witham. *Essx* 2B **40**
Witham on the Hill.
    Linc 1B **12**
Withergate. *Norf* 3B **10**
Withermarsh Green.
    Suff 3D **33**
Withersdale Street.
    Suff 1B **26**
Withersfield. *Suff* 2D **31**
Witnesham. *Suff* 1A **34**
Wittering. *Pet* 2B **12**
Witton. *Norf* 2C **19**
Witton Bridge. *Norf* 2C **11**
Wivenhoe. *Essx* 1D **41**
Wiveton. *Norf* 1D **9**
Wix. *Essx* 1A **42**
Wixoe. *Suff* 2A **32**
Woburn. *Beds* 3A **28**
Woburn Sands. *Mil* 3A **28**
Wolferton. *Norf* 3D **7**
Wollaston. *Nptn* 3A **20**
Wolterton. *Norf* 2A **10**
Woodbastwick. *Norf* 1C **19**
Woodbridge. *Suff* 2B **34**
Wood Dalling. *Norf* 3D **9**
Woodditton. *Cambs* 1D **31**
Wood End. *Beds* 3B **20**
Wood End. *Herts* 1A **38**
Woodend Green. *Essx* . . . 1C **39**
Woodford. *Nptn* 2A **20**
Woodgate. *Norf* 1D **17**
Woodham Ferrers.
    Essx 3A **40**
Woodham Mortimer.
    Essx 3B **40**
Woodham Walter. *Essx* . . 3B **40**
Woodhurst. *Cambs* 2A **22**
Woodnewton. *Nptn* 3B **12**
Woodnook. *Linc* 2A **4**
Wood Norton. *Norf* 3D **9**
Woodrising. *Norf* 2C **17**
Woodside. *Herts* 3D **37**
Woodston. *Pet* 3C **13**
Woodton. *Norf* 3B **18**
Woodwalton. *Cambs* 1D **21**
Woolley. *Cambs* 2C **21**
Woolmer Green. *Herts* . . . 2D **37**

Woolpit. *Suff* 3C **25**
Woolsthorpe. *Linc* 3A **4**
Woolverstone. *Suff* 3A **34**
Wootton. *Beds* 2B **28**
Workhouse Green. *Suff* . . . 3C **33**
Worlingham. *Suff* 3D **19**
Worlington. *Suff* 2D **23**
Worlingworth. *Suff* 3B **26**
Wormegay. *Norf* 1D **15**
Wormingford. *Essx* 3C **33**
Wormley. *Herts* 3A **38**
Worstead. *Norf* 3C **11**
Wortham. *Suff* 2D **25**
Worthing. *Norf* 1C **17**
Wortwell. *Norf* 1B **26**
Wothorpe. *Nptn* 2B **12**
Wrabness. *Essx* 3A **34**
Wramplingham. *Norf* 2A **18**
Wrangle. *Linc* 1B **6**
Wrangle Lowgate. *Linc* . . . 1B **6**
Wreningham. *Norf* 3A **18**
Wrentham. *Suff* 1D **27**
Wrestlingworth. *Beds* 2D **29**
Wretham. *Norf* 3C **17**
Wretton. *Norf* 3D **15**
Wright's Green. *Essx* 2C **39**
Writtle. *Essx* 3D **39**
Wroxham. *Norf* 1C **19**
Wyatt's Green. *Essx* 3C **39**
Wyberton. *Linc* 1A **6**
Wyboston. *Beds* 1C **29**
Wyddial. *Herts* 3A **30**
Wykeham. *Linc* 3D **5**
Wymington. *Beds* 3A **20**
Wymondham. *Leics* 1A **12**
Wymondham. *Norf* 2A **18**
Wyton. *Cambs* 2D **21**
Wyverstone. *Suff* 3D **25**
Wyverstone Street.
    Suff 3D **25**
Wyville. *Linc* 3A **4**

Y

Yardley Hastings. *Nptn* . . . 1A **28**
Yarwell. *Nptn* 3B **12**
Yaxham. *Norf* 1D **17**
Yaxley. *Cambs* 3C **13**
Yaxley. *Suff* 2A **26**
Yelden. *Beds* 3B **20**
Yelling. *Cambs* 3D **21**
Yelverton. *Norf* 2B **18**
Young's End. *Essx* 2A **40**
Yoxford. *Suff* 3C **27**

CITY & TOWN CENTRE PLANS

Bedford	56	Ely	58	Norwich	59
Bury St. Edmunds	56	Great Yarmouth	58	Peterborough	59
Cambridge	57	Ipswich	58	Harwich Port Plan	60
Chelmsford	57	King's Lynn	58	London Stansted Airport	60
Colchester	57	Luton	59		

Reference to Town Plans

MOTORWAY	**M1**
MOTORWAY UNDER CONSTRUCTION	
MOTORWAY JUNCTIONS WITH NUMBERS	**4** **5**
Unlimited Interchange **4**	
Limited Interchange **5**	
PRIMARY ROUTE	**A14**
PRIMARY ROUTE JUNCTION WITH NUMBER	**61**
DUAL CARRIAGEWAYS	
CLASS A ROAD	A143
CLASS B ROAD	B1113
MAJOR ROADS UNDER CONSTRUCTION	
MAJOR ROADS PROPOSED	
MINOR ROADS	
RESTRICTED ACCESS	
PEDESTRIANIZED ROAD & MAIN FOOTWAY	
ONE WAY STREETS	→
TOLL	TOLL
RAILWAY AND B.R. STATION	
UNDERGROUND / METRO & D.L.R. STATION	**DLR**
LEVEL CROSSING AND TUNNEL	
TRAM STOP AND ONE WAY TRAM STOP	
BUILT-UP AREA	
ABBEY, CATHEDRAL, PRIORY ETC.	✝

BUS STATION	
CAR PARK (Selection of)	P
CHURCH	†
CITY WALL	
FERRY (Vehicular)	
(Foot only)	
GOLF COURSE	
HELIPORT	
HOSPITAL	**H**
INFORMATION CENTRE	
LIGHTHOUSE	
MARKET	
NATIONAL TRUST PROPERTY (Open)	NT
(Restricted opening)	NT
(National Trust of Scotland)	NTS NTS
PARK & RIDE	
PLACE OF INTEREST	■
POLICE STATION	▲
POST OFFICE	★
SHOPPING AREA (Main street and precinct)	
SHOPMOBILITY	
TOILET	▽
VIEWPOINT	

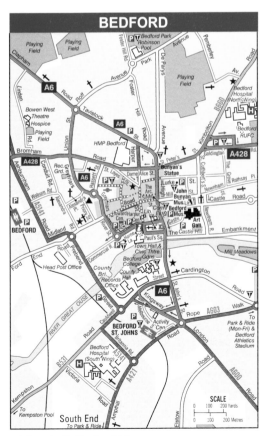

BEDFORD

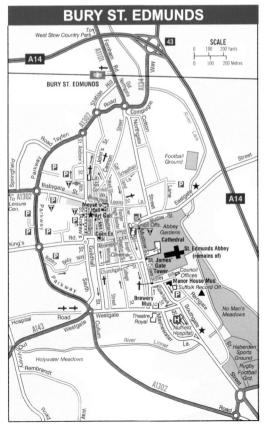

BURY ST. EDMUNDS

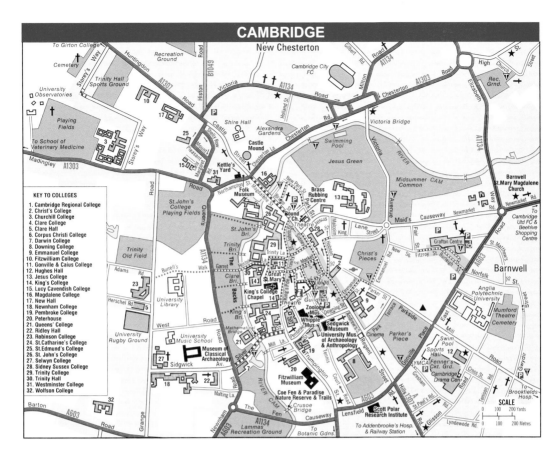

CAMBRIDGE

KEY TO COLLEGES
1. Cambridge Regional College
2. Christ's College
3. Churchill College
4. Clare College
5. Clare Hall
6. Corpus Christi College
7. Darwin College
8. Downing College
9. Emmanuel College
10. Fitzwilliam College
11. Gonville & Caius College
12. Hughes Hall
13. Jesus College
14. King's College
15. Lucy Cavendish College
16. Magdalene College
17. New Hall
18. Newnham College
19. Pembroke College
20. Peterhouse
21. Queens' College
22. Ridley Hall
23. Robinson College
24. St.Catharine's College
25. St.Edmund's College
26. St. John's College
27. Selwyn College
28. Sidney Sussex College
29. Trinity College
30. Trinity Hall
31. Westminster College
32. Wolfson College

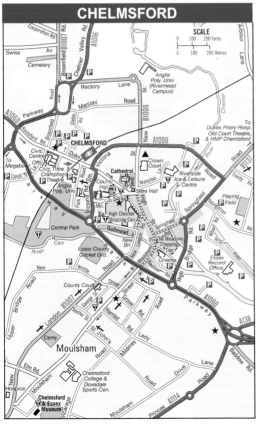

CHELMSFORD

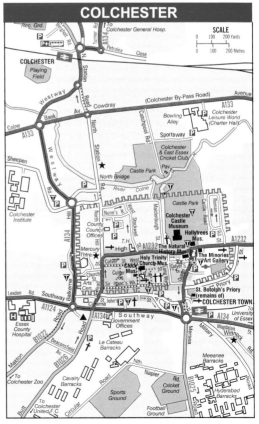

COLCHESTER

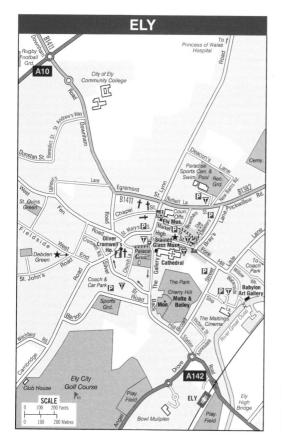

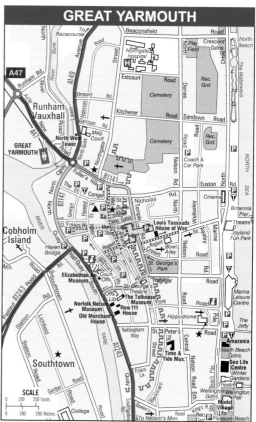

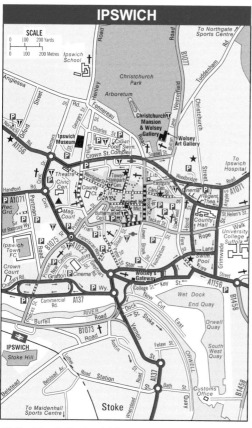

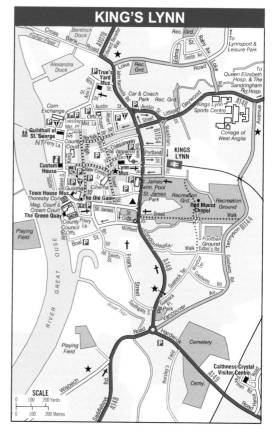

NORWICH

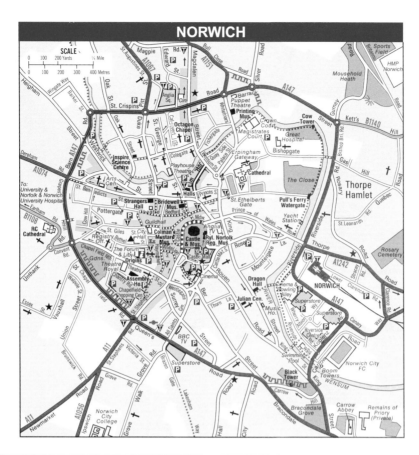

LUTON

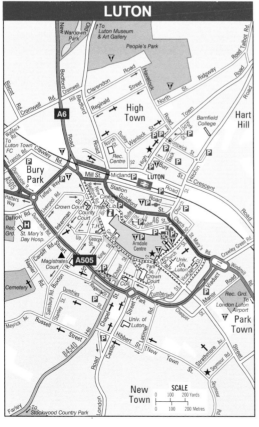

PETERBOROUGH

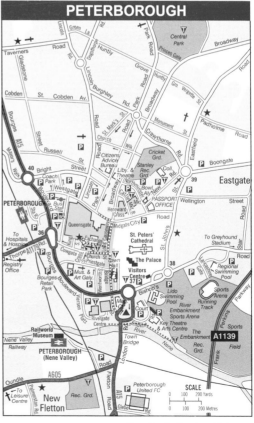

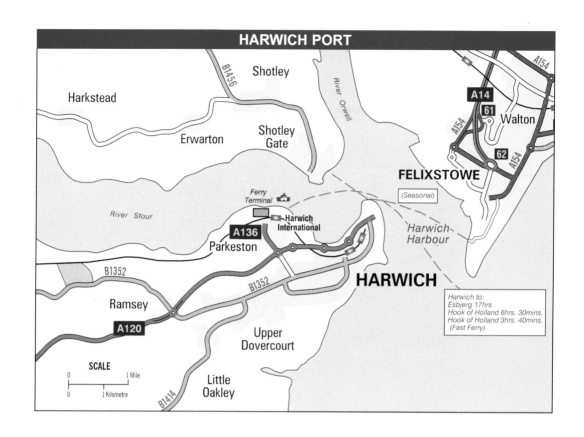

HARWICH PORT

Harkstead

Shotley

River Orwell

B1456

Erwarton

Shotley Gate

A14

61

Walton

A154

A154

A154

62

FELIXSTOWE

Ferry Terminal

(Seasonal)

River Stour

Harwich International

A136

Harwich Harbour

Parkeston

HARWICH

Harwich to:
Esbjerg 17hrs.
Hook of Holland 6hrs. 30mins.
Hook of Holland 3hrs. 40mins.
(Fast Ferry)

Ramsey

B1352

B1352

A120

Upper Dovercourt

SCALE

0 ___ 1 Mile

0 ___ 1 Kilometre

Little Oakley

B1414

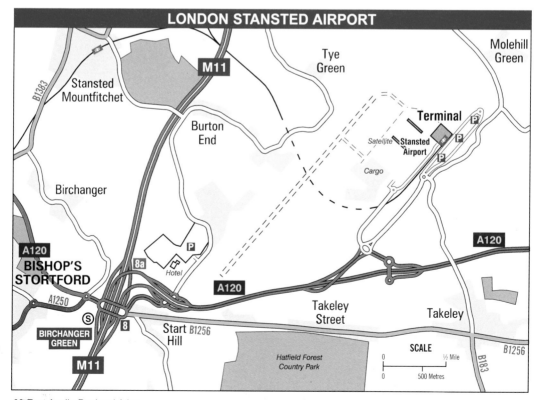

LONDON STANSTED AIRPORT

B1383

Stansted Mountfitchet

M11

Tye Green

Molehill Green

Burton End

Terminal

P

P

Satellite Stansted Airport

P

Cargo

Birchanger

A120

A120

A120

BISHOP'S STORTFORD

8a

Hotel

P

A1250

S

8

BIRCHANGER GREEN

M11

Start Hill

B1256

Takeley Street

Takeley

Hatfield Forest Country Park

SCALE

0 ___ ½ Mile

0 ___ 500 Metres

B183

B1256

60 East Anglia Regional Atlas